THIS
BOOK
IS
DANGEROUS

A READING JOURNAL

(for those who don't want to be told
what they can—or can't—read)

NICOLE LINTEMUTH

Media Lab Books
For inquiries, contact customerservice@topixmedia.com

Copyright 2024 Nicole Lintemuth

Published by Topix Media Lab
14 Wall Street, Suite 3C
New York, NY 10005

Printed in China

ISBN-13: 978-1-956403-74-9
ISBN-10: 1-956403-74-4

For every librarian, teacher and author
who's ever helped someone feel more seen, understood
and powerful through the gift of reading.

Introduction

WHEN I WAS growing up in Michigan's Upper Peninsula in the 1990s, I had no idea that "bisexual" was a thing. I knew what straight was, I knew what gay was and I knew I was neither of those things.

As I got older (and thanks to the internet), I finally found the language for who I am, and it changed my life. I wasn't alone, a freak or broken in any way.

I was in my 30s before I finally got to read a book from a major publisher that featured a bisexual main character (*Red, White & Royal Blue* by Casey McQuiston). It was a little while later before I was able to read a book with a bisexual woman as the main character (*The Lady's Guide to Celestial Mechanics* by Olivia Waite), and it was even later that I was able to read a book with a bisexual/queer woman main character who was in a relationship with a cis/het man (*Take a Hint, Dani Brown* by Talia Hibbert).

It wasn't until I was finally able to see myself reflected in a book that I realized how badly I had needed that form of representation.

As an Air Force veteran, I still hold the core values: Integrity First, Service Before Self, and Excellence in All We Do. Those ideas form a central part of who I am. So when I opened my bookstore, Bettie's Pages, in 2020, I knew my goal was to allow others to see themselves on the shelf a lot earlier than I did. This decision, perhaps inevitably, put me in direct conflict with those who challenge and ban books or who seek to diminish or erase incredibly valuable representation.

Books are powerful. They can open your mind, give you language and understanding and, most importantly, give you the tools to change the world. This makes them a danger to those who are invested in keeping folks in the dark.

I hope you'll use this book journal to record all your reads. That's its purpose! But I also hope it will teach you more about your power in the fight against censorship, help you find amazing reads you might not have heard of before and lead you on a journey that will make your own bookshelf a little more diverse!

Happy Reading!
Nicole

What's in a Ban?

Book bans explained in brief, from the challenge to (maybe) the Supreme Court.

AS LONG AS there have been books in the world, there have been people determined to dictate what others can read. Despite there being advances in Gutenberg's method, sometimes it can feel like we're stuck in an age that predates the Enlightenment—especially when it seems like every day brings another news story about a new challenge, ban or piece of legislation that limits the knowledge available to the public. But I truly believe

that we have the power to fight back and protect our right to read.

Most people don't pay a lot of attention to school board, library board or city council meetings until things have gone sideways and a local governing body has started challenging or banning books. Most of these efforts happen at the hyper-local level; a book may get challenged and banned in one school district but be required reading one district over.

We also know the majority of challenges and bans never even get reported, let alone make the news. After all, the minutes of a school board meeting are unlikely to garner airtime from your network anchor. The American Library Association tracks challenges and bans in libraries across the country through a self-report system and through what data is reported by the media. But according to their estimates, they only hear about 10 percent of all the bans and challenges each year. This means a staggering 90 percent never make the news and never have an opportunity to be fought against.

Bans and challenges thrive in environments where secrecy, confusion and disempowerment thrive. Don't lose hope,

I'm here to help give you the language and tools to confidently protect books in your community!

HOW DO BOOK BANS WORK?

Bans generally start with a challenge, when someone walks into a library and says "I don't like this book and think you should get rid of it." Sometimes they invoke God. Other times they name-drop Satan. Most often—especially these days—they beg you to "THINK OF THE CHILDREN." A challenge can happen at a public library, school library, university or research library: Heck, people will try to challenge books in places where they have no official say, such as city council meetings or bookstores. If a challenge is accepted, it evolves into a ban, which means the challenged book is no longer accessible to the public from that source.

Every library will have its own process for handling challenges, (and if they don't, they need one ASAP!). Some will have a public committee read and review the book. In schools, this task often falls to different stakeholders such as administration, teachers, parents and community members. Other libraries will review the book internally. Unfortunately, some libraries don't even put up a fight—defending the book is deemed too costly (in terms of time, political capital or actual funds) and so the book is pulled immediately.

Don't worry though: this isn't the end of that book's story. Even if a book is banned, that doesn't have to be the end of the fight. Book challenges and bans have been appealed all the way to the Supreme Court multiple times, and so far, the court has upheld our freedom to read each time—fingers crossed it stays that way!

> **Between January and August 2023, 11 states challenged more than 100 books each, according to the American Library Association.**

According to *Encyclopedia Britannica*, in 1900, a U.S. school prohibited Lewis Carroll's *Alice's Adventures in Wonderland* from its curriculum, claiming that it expressed expletives and alluded to masturbation and other sexual fantasies as well as diminished— in the eyes of children—the statures of certain authority figures.

WHERE ARE BOOKS BANNED?

Challenges happen most often in public libraries (48 percent) and school libraries (41 percent), but as I said earlier, they can happen anywhere books are housed. PEN America is an organization that defends the freedom of writers, artists and journalists and protects free expression worldwide. Like the ALA, it also tracks book bans and challenges, specifically in schools. The data from the two organizations makes it clear that book challenges and bans are happening everywhere. Red states and blue ones. Big cities and small towns. Rich counties and poor ones. It doesn't matter where you live: Book bans and challenges are happening within driving distance of you right now.

WHO IS BANNING BOOKS?

Most often, the folks banning books are exactly the type you imagine: right-wing, often religious conservatives. Since 2020, when the killing of George Floyd brought the idea of critical race theory into the mainstream media, books have become a cultural wedge issue. While the vast majority of bans are instituted by conservatives, they're not the only ones.

Folks have challenged the Bible enough that it's on the ALA's Top 100 Most Banned and Challenged Books: 2010-2019 list. People challenge books for racist or sexist content or just ideas they deem dangerous and inappropriate. While those making

CENSORED

challenges may feel justified in their approach, banning books is never the answer.

WHAT IS BEING BANNED?

Today, the books most often challenged and banned are ones that feature LGBTQIA+ content and books with BIPOC characters and authors. Those are pretty broad categories, so let's unpack them a bit.

LGBTQIA+ content can mean anything including nonfiction books about gender identity and sexuality, memoirs by LGBTQIA+ folks or simple board books explaining what pronouns are. It also includes fiction books that feature LGBTQIA+ main characters, the exploration of identity or even a single image of same-sex parents in a picture book.

Starting in 2020, the number of books challenged or banned related to anti-racism, BIPOC characters or depictions of police violence skyrocketed. These two categories make up the vast majority

of book challenges. But you'll often hear the same reasoning given for these challenges. Banners argue that the books are inappropriate, divisive, dangerous and confusing for kids to read.

Books that feature sexual content (straight or queer), religious minorities or even common swears also garnered challenges. And that's a damn shame.

According to the American Library Association, a record 2,571 unique titles were targeted for censorship in 2022, a 38 percent increase over the 1,858 unique titles targeted for censorship in 2021.

Legislation Tracker

A handy place to keep track of any pending legislation that might affect your local libraries or schools.

A GROWING NUMBER of states and local governments have been using legislation as a way to attack books. But remember: Legislators work for us. You shouldn't be afraid to speak up if your representatives aren't doing their jobs. The first step is knowing exactly who they are by using the representative contact information you gather on pg. 187. Then do all you can to stay up to date on what they're doing.

This tracker will help if you are in an area where anti-book legislation is being proposed. To get more information and learn more about ways to get involved, connect with your state library association or ACLU office!

From July 2021 to June 2022, PEN America's Index of School Book Bans lists 2,532 instances of individual books being banned, affecting 1,648 unique book titles.

LEGISLATION _____ DATE INTRODUCED _____

PROPOSED BY _____ LOCATION _____

IMPACT IT WOULD HAVE _____

WHY YOU SUPPORT OR OPPOSE IT _____

REPRESENTATIVE CONTACTED _____ DATE_____

CONTACT METHOD _____ RESPONSE _____

_____

REPRESENTATIVE CONTACTED _____ DATE_____

CONTACT METHOD _____ RESPONSE _____

_____

REPRESENTATIVE CONTACTED _____ DATE_____

CONTACT METHOD _____ RESPONSE _____

_____

PROPOSAL	HEARING	1ST VOTE	2ND VOTE	SIGNED/ VETOED	LAW	

LEGISLATION _____ DATE INTRODUCED _____

PROPOSED BY _____ LOCATION _____

IMPACT IT WOULD HAVE _____

WHY YOU SUPPORT OR OPPOSE IT _____

REPRESENTATIVE CONTACTED _____ DATE_____

CONTACT METHOD _____ RESPONSE _____

_____

REPRESENTATIVE CONTACTED _____ DATE_____

CONTACT METHOD _____ RESPONSE _____

_____

REPRESENTATIVE CONTACTED _____ DATE_____

CONTACT METHOD _____ RESPONSE _____

_____

PROPOSAL	HEARING	1ST VOTE	2ND VOTE	SIGNED/ VETOED	LAW	

LEGISLATION _____ DATE INTRODUCED _____

PROPOSED BY _____ LOCATION _____

IMPACT IT WOULD HAVE _____

WHY YOU SUPPORT OR OPPOSE IT _____

REPRESENTATIVE CONTACTED _____ DATE_____

CONTACT METHOD _____ RESPONSE _____

_____

REPRESENTATIVE CONTACTED _____ DATE_____

CONTACT METHOD _____ RESPONSE _____

_____

REPRESENTATIVE CONTACTED _____ DATE_____

CONTACT METHOD _____ RESPONSE _____

_____

PROPOSAL	HEARING	1ST VOTE	2ND VOTE	SIGNED/ VETOED	LAW	

LEGISLATION _____ DATE INTRODUCED _____

PROPOSED BY _____ LOCATION _____

IMPACT IT WOULD HAVE _____

WHY YOU SUPPORT OR OPPOSE IT _____

REPRESENTATIVE CONTACTED _____ DATE_____

CONTACT METHOD _____ RESPONSE _____

_____

REPRESENTATIVE CONTACTED _____ DATE_____

CONTACT METHOD _____ RESPONSE _____

_____

REPRESENTATIVE CONTACTED _____ DATE_____

CONTACT METHOD _____ RESPONSE _____

_____

PROPOSAL	HEARING	1ST VOTE	2ND VOTE	SIGNED/ VETOED	LAW	

LEGISLATION _____ DATE INTRODUCED _____

PROPOSED BY _____ LOCATION _____

IMPACT IT WOULD HAVE _____

WHY YOU SUPPORT OR OPPOSE IT _____

REPRESENTATIVE CONTACTED _____ DATE_____

CONTACT METHOD _____ RESPONSE _____

_____

REPRESENTATIVE CONTACTED _____ DATE_____

CONTACT METHOD _____ RESPONSE _____

_____

REPRESENTATIVE CONTACTED _____ DATE_____

CONTACT METHOD _____ RESPONSE _____

_____

PROPOSAL	HEARING	1ST VOTE	2ND VOTE	SIGNED/ VETOED	LAW	

LEGISLATION _____ DATE INTRODUCED _____

PROPOSED BY _____ LOCATION _____

IMPACT IT WOULD HAVE _____

WHY YOU SUPPORT OR OPPOSE IT _____

REPRESENTATIVE CONTACTED _____ DATE_____

CONTACT METHOD _____ RESPONSE _____

_____

REPRESENTATIVE CONTACTED _____ DATE_____

CONTACT METHOD _____ RESPONSE _____

_____

REPRESENTATIVE CONTACTED _____ DATE_____

CONTACT METHOD _____ RESPONSE _____

_____

PROPOSAL	HEARING	1ST VOTE	2ND VOTE	SIGNED/ VETOED	LAW	

LEGISLATION _____ DATE INTRODUCED _____

PROPOSED BY _____ LOCATION _____

IMPACT IT WOULD HAVE _____

WHY YOU SUPPORT OR OPPOSE IT _____

REPRESENTATIVE CONTACTED _____ DATE_____

CONTACT METHOD _____ RESPONSE _____

_____

REPRESENTATIVE CONTACTED _____ DATE_____

CONTACT METHOD _____ RESPONSE _____

_____

REPRESENTATIVE CONTACTED _____ DATE_____

CONTACT METHOD _____ RESPONSE _____

_____

PROPOSAL	HEARING	1ST VOTE	2ND VOTE	SIGNED/ VETOED	LAW	

LEGISLATION _____ DATE INTRODUCED _____

PROPOSED BY _____ LOCATION _____

IMPACT IT WOULD HAVE _____

WHY YOU SUPPORT OR OPPOSE IT _____

REPRESENTATIVE CONTACTED _____ DATE_____

CONTACT METHOD _____ RESPONSE _____

_____

REPRESENTATIVE CONTACTED _____ DATE_____

CONTACT METHOD _____ RESPONSE _____

_____

REPRESENTATIVE CONTACTED _____ DATE_____

CONTACT METHOD _____ RESPONSE _____

_____

PROPOSAL	HEARING	1ST VOTE	2ND VOTE	SIGNED/ VETOED	LAW	

LEGISLATION _____ DATE INTRODUCED _____

PROPOSED BY _____ LOCATION _____

IMPACT IT WOULD HAVE _____

WHY YOU SUPPORT OR OPPOSE IT _____

REPRESENTATIVE CONTACTED _____ DATE_____

CONTACT METHOD _____ RESPONSE _____

_____

REPRESENTATIVE CONTACTED _____ DATE_____

CONTACT METHOD _____ RESPONSE _____

_____

REPRESENTATIVE CONTACTED _____ DATE_____

CONTACT METHOD _____ RESPONSE _____

_____

PROPOSAL	HEARING	1ST VOTE	2ND VOTE	SIGNED/ VETOED	LAW	

LEGISLATION _____ DATE INTRODUCED _____

PROPOSED BY _____ LOCATION _____

IMPACT IT WOULD HAVE _____

WHY YOU SUPPORT OR OPPOSE IT _____

REPRESENTATIVE CONTACTED _____ DATE_____

CONTACT METHOD _____ RESPONSE _____

_____

REPRESENTATIVE CONTACTED _____ DATE_____

CONTACT METHOD _____ RESPONSE _____

_____

REPRESENTATIVE CONTACTED _____ DATE_____

CONTACT METHOD _____ RESPONSE _____

_____

PROPOSAL	HEARING	1ST VOTE	2ND VOTE	SIGNED/ VETOED	LAW	

LEGISLATION _____ DATE INTRODUCED _____

PROPOSED BY _____ LOCATION _____

IMPACT IT WOULD HAVE _____

WHY YOU SUPPORT OR OPPOSE IT _____

REPRESENTATIVE CONTACTED _____ DATE_____

CONTACT METHOD _____ RESPONSE _____

_____

REPRESENTATIVE CONTACTED _____ DATE_____

CONTACT METHOD _____ RESPONSE _____

_____

REPRESENTATIVE CONTACTED _____ DATE_____

CONTACT METHOD _____ RESPONSE _____

_____

PROPOSAL	HEARING	1ST VOTE	2ND VOTE	SIGNED/ VETOED	LAW	

LEGISLATION _____ **DATE INTRODUCED** _____

PROPOSED BY _____ **LOCATION** _____

IMPACT IT WOULD HAVE _____

WHY YOU SUPPORT OR OPPOSE IT _____

REPRESENTATIVE CONTACTED _____ **DATE** _____

CONTACT METHOD _____ **RESPONSE** _____

_____

REPRESENTATIVE CONTACTED _____ **DATE** _____

CONTACT METHOD _____ **RESPONSE** _____

_____

REPRESENTATIVE CONTACTED _____ **DATE** _____

CONTACT METHOD _____ **RESPONSE** _____

_____

PROPOSAL	HEARING	1ST VOTE	2ND VOTE	SIGNED/ VETOED	LAW	

LEGISLATION _____ **DATE INTRODUCED** _____

PROPOSED BY _____ **LOCATION** _____

IMPACT IT WOULD HAVE _____

WHY YOU SUPPORT OR OPPOSE IT _____

REPRESENTATIVE CONTACTED _____ **DATE** _____

CONTACT METHOD _____ **RESPONSE** _____

_____

REPRESENTATIVE CONTACTED _____ **DATE** _____

CONTACT METHOD _____ **RESPONSE** _____

_____

REPRESENTATIVE CONTACTED _____ **DATE** _____

CONTACT METHOD _____ **RESPONSE** _____

_____

PROPOSAL	HEARING	1ST VOTE	2ND VOTE	SIGNED/ VETOED	LAW	

LEGISLATION _____ DATE INTRODUCED _____

PROPOSED BY _____ LOCATION _____

IMPACT IT WOULD HAVE _____

WHY YOU SUPPORT OR OPPOSE IT _____

REPRESENTATIVE CONTACTED _____ DATE_____

CONTACT METHOD _____ RESPONSE _____

_____

REPRESENTATIVE CONTACTED _____ DATE_____

CONTACT METHOD _____ RESPONSE _____

_____

REPRESENTATIVE CONTACTED _____ DATE_____

CONTACT METHOD _____ RESPONSE _____

_____

PROPOSAL	HEARING	1ST VOTE	2ND VOTE	SIGNED/ VETOED	LAW	

LEGISLATION _____ DATE INTRODUCED _____

PROPOSED BY _____ LOCATION _____

IMPACT IT WOULD HAVE _____

WHY YOU SUPPORT OR OPPOSE IT _____

REPRESENTATIVE CONTACTED _____ DATE_____

CONTACT METHOD _____ RESPONSE _____

_____

REPRESENTATIVE CONTACTED _____ DATE_____

CONTACT METHOD _____ RESPONSE _____

_____

REPRESENTATIVE CONTACTED _____ DATE_____

CONTACT METHOD _____ RESPONSE _____

_____

PROPOSAL	HEARING	1ST VOTE	2ND VOTE	SIGNED/ VETOED	LAW	

KNOW YOUR ENEMY
Gain a deeper understanding of bans so you can fight for your right to read.

ONE QUESTION I get a lot when talking about book bans is "How do we argue for books that people are calling obscene or pornographic? Of course I don't want kids reading that!"

The first thing I tell them in the ensuing debate is that knowledge is power. Understanding what is obscene according to the First Amendment is a great place to start. Secondly, all politics are local. Make sure your representatives know where you stand and get comfortable showing up to meetings. But there are also a number of legal precedents that cover the right to read as protected by the First Amendment. What follows is a brief breakdown of some of the most useful examples to bring up when faced with someone who believes banning books is the best solution to complicated questions.

Let's start with the definition of "obscene," because this word gets thrown around a lot. But despite the popular saying, this isn't an "I know it when I see it" situation. There is an actual legal definition based on the Miller Test, detailed here:

In Miller v. California (1973), the Supreme Court established the Miller Test to determine what is or is not obscene. To be considered obscene, materials must meet all three parts of this test:

1. Whether an average person would find that the work, on the whole, appeals to the prurient (sexual) interest.
2. Whether the work depicts or describes, in a patently offensive way, sexual conduct specifically defined by the applicable state law.
3. Whether the work, taken as a whole, lacks serious literary, artistic, political or scientific value.

Knowledge of precedents like these is helpful for empowering people. But when it comes to forming what you plan to say to representatives or during public comment time, I find that the biggest impact comes from sharing how these books and others like them have influenced your life. At the end of the day, people respond to the personal. And while it's helpful to have some knowledge of the

Bans Throughout History

On multiple occasions, the Supreme Court has affirmed the right to read and that censorship is a violation of the First Amendment. Here are a few more cases that have defined and protected those rights:

- **Smith v. California (1959)**

The Supreme Court found that a California law banning the sale of "obscene" books was too vague and violated the First Amendment right to freedom of speech.

- **Board of Education, Island Trees Union Free School District v. Pico (1982)**

This case determined that schools may not remove books from the library based solely on partisan or political grounds. This means they can't ban a whole category of books (e.g., LGBTQIA+). Each book banned must have a specific and valid reason that isn't political/partisan.

These are a few examples of Supreme Court cases protecting books, but this barely scratches the surface. More recent cases include:

- **Case v. Unified School District No. 233 (1995)**
- **Sund v. City of Wichita Falls (2000)**
- **Counts v. Cedarville School District (2003)**

---

legal nitty gritty, citations can get dry pretty quickly.

And don't be afraid to get the kids involved: They have just as much right to knowledge as adults do, and they will be the ones most impacted by book bans. Their voices are compelling and should be encouraged.

Books are powerful and often can challenge folks to reflect on, and sometimes reevaluate, ideas they've always held. For those who wish to ban books, that's scary. For the rest of us, that's the point! Talk about this, especially if you're a parent. It's also helpful to talk about your right to determine what your child reads and that no one else has the right to do that for you.

Lastly, I encourage folks to take a stand and demand more books with diverse representation. Too often, it feels that anti-ban folks are begging to preserve the few diverse books we do have. The next generation deserves the ability to learn and grow. They're going to encounter a variety of people in the world: Books can open this world up to them in a unique way!

It can feel like you're arguing with a brick wall when talking to folks in favor of bans. Don't waste time with people who aren't interested in learning. Focus on fence-sitters and public officials who have shown a willingness to stand with books.

TO RECAP:

1. Knowledge is power. Know what rights you have and who can help.

2. Make it personal. Don't let them make decisions without knowing where you stand.

3. Don't give up! The numbers are on our side. Seventy one percent of people believe it's wrong to ban books. We just need to keep showing up and speaking up!

NAMING AND SHAMING

The groups fighting against your right to read: Who they are and what they believe.

ACCORDING TO THE American Library Association, prior to 2021, most book challenges were aimed at a single title. This changed dramatically in 2022 when 90 percent of challenges listed more than one book at a time. Why is that?

It's due, in large part, to the fact that certain groups across the United States have decided to use books as their cultural wedge issue, making books a means to defund schools and libraries and push an agenda of hate toward LGBTQIA+, BIPOC and other marginalized communities.

PEN America found that in the 2021-2022 school year, more than 50 advocacy groups across the country were directly responsible for 20 percent of bans in schools, with an additional 30 percent of the bans strongly influenced by these groups.

So who are these people? What follows is not a comprehensive list, but these are some of the biggest names coming into our communities to try to ban books.

⊘ MOMS FOR LIBERTY

A conservative advocacy group with chapters across the country focused on fighting against school curricula that mention LGBTQIA+ rights, critical race theory, discrimination and race and ethnicity. Started in 2021 in Broward County, Florida, by two former school board members, the group has been labeled an extremist organization by the Southern Poverty Law Center for its social media posts, policies and practices, which target teachers, administrators and librarians. They advance a variety of conspiracy theories and spread hateful anti-LGBTQIA+ imagery and rhetoric.

⊘ NO LEFT TURN IN EDUCATION

Founded in the summer of 2020, this group has become a leading faction in the fight against what they perceive as critical race theory (CRT)—the idea that racism and discrimination are a feature of American culture, not a bug—in the K–12 curriculum. CRT is a graduate-level concept that is not taught at the K–12 level anywhere in the U.S. No Left Turn claims wins in states that have proposed and/or passed legislation prohibiting the teaching of the concept...but it was never being taught anyway! They have become well known for their disruptive and aggressive tactics at school board meetings across the country. They provide resources, template letters and other tools to members to replicate efforts across the country to recall school board members, ban books and influence legislators.

⊘ MASSRESISTANCE

Founded in 1995 in Waltham, Massachusetts, this group was originally known as Parents' Rights Coalition and was formed to oppose same-sex marriage before it was legalized in Massachusetts in 2004. The organization changed its name to MassResistance in 2006

According to the American Library Association, *in July 2023, the* Des Moines Register *obtained a list of 374 books that Urbandale (Iowa) Community School District had flagged for removal without knowing if the district even owned the books as organized right-wing efforts to produce book ban lists intensified.*

and continues to fight against LGBTQIA+ equality. They have been designated as an anti-LGBTQIA+ hate group by the Southern Poverty Law Center and have chapters across the country that continue to perpetuate conspiracy theories against anti-racist groups such as Black Lives Matter and use their platforms to lie about "dangers" posed by the LGBTQIA+ community.

⊘ PARENTS DEFENDING EDUCATION (PDE)

A conservative 501(c)3 nonprofit organization based in Virginia, this group claims to be a grassroots movement to fight back against "woke indoctrination" in schools, but is actually funded by the Koch brothers and other conservative dark money organizations.

With strong ties to the American Legislative Exchange Council (ALEC), it supports legislative and school policy-based efforts to ban books that include content about gender identity, sexuality, critical race theory, mental health or critical social commentary.

These organizations, and others like them, have created resources for banning books that have been shared via social media with local groups across the country. These lists make it easier for people to challenge books en masse. They list the book as well as pages to reference, allowing like-minded locals to copy and paste reasons for their challenges.

We're also seeing explosive growth in legislative efforts to ban books and censor schools and libraries. Right-wing conservative legislators across the country have filed more than 145 bills to restrict access to books.

EveryLibrary, an organization that promotes and advocates for public funding for libraries, created a tracker of legislation by state. Check who's proposed legislation in your state: *everylibrary.org/billtracking*.

My Outlaw Library: Book #1

"Censorship reflects a society's lack of confidence in itself."

—Potter Stewart, Associate Justice of the U.S. Supreme Court (1915–1985)

BOOK_____

AUTHOR_____

GENRE_____ DATE FINISHED_____

RATE THE FOLLOWING (1–10):

Characters _____ Plot/Narrative _____ Illustrations (if applicable) _____

HOW I READ IT   ☐ Print   ☐ Audiobook   ☐ eBook

WHERE I GOT IT   ☐ Bookstore   ☐ Library   ☐ Friend   ☐ Other

MOODS/VIBES

1._____

2._____

3._____

4._____

5._____

REPRESENTATION

☐ BIPOC ☐ LGBTQIA+ ☐ Immigrant ☐ Disability ☐ Neurodiversity ☐ Other_____

ASK YOURSELF

What made me pick up this book? _____

_____

_____

_____

_____

Did it deliver? How so? _____

_____

_____

Would I recommend this book? Why or Why not? _____

_____

_____

If so, to whom? _____

_____

What was the best quote or idea I got from this book? _____

_____

_____

_____

_____

_____

If someone challenged this book, what reason do I *think* they would give? _____

_____

_____

_____

_____

Has it been challenged? If so, was it banned, and for what reason? _____

_____

_____

_____

_____

_____

What would I say to people who want to ban this book? _____

_____

_____

_____

_____

_____

_____

My Outlaw Library: Book #2
Hungry? Feed your head.

BOOK_____

AUTHOR_____

GENRE_____ DATE FINISHED_____

RATE THE FOLLOWING (1–10):

Characters _____ Plot/Narrative _____ Illustrations (if applicable) _____

HOW I READ IT □ Print □ Audiobook □ eBook

WHERE I GOT IT □ Bookstore □ Library □ Friend □ Other

MOODS/VIBES

1._____

2._____

3._____

4._____

5._____

REPRESENTATION

□ BIPOC □ LGBTQIA+ □ Immigrant □ Disability □ Neurodiversity □ Other_____

ASK YOURSELF

What made me pick up this book? _____

_____

_____

_____

_____

Did it deliver? How so? _____
_____
_____

Would I recommend this book? Why or Why not? _____
_____
_____

If so, to whom? _____
_____

What was the best quote or idea I got from this book? _____
_____
_____
_____
_____

If someone challenged this book, what reason do I *think* they would give? ___
_____
_____
_____

Has it been challenged? If so, was it banned, and for what reason? _____
_____
_____
_____
_____

What would I say to people who want to ban this book? _____
_____
_____
_____
_____
_____

My Outlaw Library: Book #3

It sounds relaxing, but curling up with a good book counts as activism these days.

BOOK _____

AUTHOR _____

GENRE _____ DATE FINISHED _____

RATE THE FOLLOWING (1–10):

Characters _____ Plot/Narrative _____ Illustrations (if applicable) _____

HOW I READ IT ☐ Print   ☐ Audiobook   ☐ eBook

WHERE I GOT IT ☐ Bookstore   ☐ Library   ☐ Friend   ☐ Other

MOODS/VIBES

1. _____
2. _____
3. _____
4. _____
5. _____

REPRESENTATION

☐ BIPOC ☐ LGBTQIA+ ☐ Immigrant ☐ Disability ☐ Neurodiversity ☐ Other_____

ASK YOURSELF

What made me pick up this book? _____

_____

_____

_____

_____

Did it deliver? How so? _____

_____

_____

Would I recommend this book? Why or Why not? _____

_____

_____

If so, to whom? _____

_____

What was the best quote or idea I got from this book? _____

_____

_____

_____

_____

If someone challenged this book, what reason do I *think* they would give? _____

_____

_____

_____

Has it been challenged? If so, was it banned, and for what reason? _____

_____

_____

_____

_____

What would I say to people who want to ban this book? _____

_____

_____

_____

_____

_____

Because They Don't Want You To (PART 1)

Whether they were banned for their inclusion of the marginalized, the questioning of authority or a half-baked combination of the two, the books that follow— along with those on pgs. 42–43, 62–63 and 74–75— deserve a place in our culture.

GRAPHIC FICTION & NONFICTION

IT IS UNFORTUNATELY very easy to pull a couple of panels from a graphic novel or nonfiction book and use them out of context to advocate for banning that book. But the immense popularity of the genre and the beautiful way authors are able to tell a story through artwork and text is exactly what makes it such a powerful medium.

☐ **GENDER QUEER** *by Maia Kobabe*
This book is a vulnerable look at Maia's (pronouns: e/em/eir) own life, growing up and discovering e is both non-binary and asexual. I learned so much from this book and I hate how often book-banners will try to present its themes as obscene. The panels they claim are explicit are actually beautiful examples of consent and boundaries in action. According to the ALA, it was the #1 most challenged book in the U.S. in 2021 and 2022 for LGBTQIA+ content and sexual explicitness.

☐ **HEY, KIDDO** *by Jarrett Krosoczka*
Jarrett's memoir of growing up with his grandparents as his mother struggled with addiction hit especially hard for me, as I am also the child of addicts. But his humor and love for his family shine through the dark parts, giving this graphic memoir just the right balance. It is regularly challenged and banned for inappropriate words, sex, drugs, alcohol and depictions of theft.

☐ **DRAMA** *by Raina Telgemeier*
If you were a theater kid, this book is for you. *Drama* will be relatable for anyone who has ever felt out of place, which I think is all of us in one way or another. And the LGBTQIA+ representation that so often gets this book challenged and banned is exactly the kind of representation kids need to see to know they're not alone in the world. Banned for LGBTQIA+ content and perceived opposition to "family values/morals."

☐ **FLAMER** *by Mike Curato*
Drawing from his own experiences as a gay

Filipino Boy Scout, Curato's graphic novel *Flamer* is beautiful: illustrated mostly in black and white, with accents of red and yellow flame, the book is visually stunning. But it is also emotionally powerful! In 2022, it was deemed pornographic by the Oklahoma Secretary of Public Education and was tied for #1 most banned or challenged book in schools alongside *Gender Queer* according to PEN America.

☐ MAUS *by Art Spiegelman*

Maus is a graphic novel-memoir. Spiegelman details his father's experience during the Holocaust, along with his own experiences as a child, to tell how the horrors of genocide can echo through generations. There is no way to tell that story in a polite way, which is precisely why it is important. A Tennessee school board banned *Maus* from its 8th-grade curriculum for animal nudity and "rough" language, though as of press time no one had insisted upon photoshopping pants onto the animals in *National Geographic*.

TONI MORRISON NOVELS

TONI MORRISON'S BOOKS have a long history of being challenged and banned. She was a Nobel Prize-winning writer for a reason—she didn't write easy books. Her work is staggering. It makes you consider things. Feel things. Confront things and react to them. And that's the point banners fail to understand. We have to engage with the ugly parts of the world; otherwise, we'll never be able to improve it.

☐ THE BLUEST EYE

Set in the pre-WWII Midwest, *The Bluest Eye* tells a story of self-hate in a world that promotes a standard of unattainable white beauty. It is regularly challenged and banned for its depictions of child sexual abuse.

☐ BELOVED

This masterpiece pulls no punches. It is hard. It is painful to read. It shines a light on parts of our history we'd much rather forget. Slavery and the scars it left behind are not easy topics to read about, and that is precisely why we need to continue to read about them. *Beloved* is challenged and banned for being sexually explicit, for its religious viewpoint and for its depictions of violence.

☐ SONG OF SOLOMON

The story of Macon "Milkman" Dead, trying to unravel his family's past while struggling with his present, this one can be a tough but also beautiful read. Much like Morrison's other books, *Song of Solomon* is an unflinching look at racism and the enduring legacy of slavery in our culture. Those are the exact reasons why people continue to challenge or ban it.

In the court case Island Trees School District v. Pico (1982), the Supreme Court ruled that school officials cannot ban books solely based on their content.

Voices of the People
Question 1: Impact

UNFORTUNATELY, MOST OF what we hear about book bans comes from large media outlets. So I collected quotes from real people whose lives, educations and livelihoods are affected by the growing culture of right-wing censorship. Book bans affect so many different groups, from writers and librarians to teachers and students, parents and booksellers. In my interviews, I found fright, outrage and anger, but also a bit of hope (thanks, students!) Beyond the groups I was able to interview, I firmly believe we are all impacted, because the denial of rights and freedoms to anyone is a blow to the rights and freedoms of us all. In Part 1, we discuss the following question:

How have book challenges/bans impacted you, your students or your institution?

I have had three years of pretty constant bullying and harassing on social media and at school board meetings. This has been mainly directed at me and has been personal, even though parents can restrict any title they would like from their child's access. It makes no sense to me.
—Anonymous Library Media Director, Lowell Area Schools

It's chilling. I've never had to second-guess what I keep in my classroom library until last year.
—Jeff, Teacher

Honestly, I didn't know that you could even ban books until my freshman year and I genuinely thought it was stupid, but no matter what I'm still able to read what I want.
—Anneliese, Student

I'm always keeping one eye on the district to see what bans or challenges might be in the works. As a queer teacher who's out in the workplace, it does make me think twice sometimes if I, for instance, read the kids a storybook where a child has queer parents or a child exhibits any kind of gender difference. People might think this doesn't impact STEM teachers, but it does. It's not as obvious as ripping *Romeo and Juliet* from the classroom. Sometimes it's "science says there are two biological sexes," which is simply untrue.

—Anna, Teacher

The biggest impact of book bans in our community has been on the readers. The books being challenged and banned in our community are those written by and about already marginalized voices, like people of color, indigenous people, immigrants or people in the LGBTQIA+ community. This not only further silences their voices, it tells these people that their voices, their opinions and their experiences do not belong in our community. It tells the kids who identify with those books and characters that they don't belong either. And kids then carry that feeling with them into adulthood. This only serves to divide us and widen the polarization within our country.

—Emily Lessig,
The Violet Fox Bookshop, Virginia

Our bookshop has been positioned as a safe place for people to get these books when they aren't available at schools. We are also on "banned" lists of our own—those who wish to limit the freedom to read won't shop at our store, if they ever did to begin with.

—Aimee, Bookseller

My Outlaw Library: Book #4

Proudly read while sipping [insert beverage here] at an outdoor table at my favorite café.

BOOK _____

AUTHOR _____

GENRE _____ DATE FINISHED _____

RATE THE FOLLOWING (1–10):

Characters _____ Plot/Narrative _____ Illustrations (if applicable) _____

HOW I READ IT   □ Print   □ Audiobook   □ eBook

WHERE I GOT IT   □ Bookstore   □ Library   □ Friend   □ Other

MOODS/VIBES

1. _____

2. _____

3. _____

4. _____

5. _____

REPRESENTATION

□ BIPOC □ LGBTQIA+ □ Immigrant □ Disability □ Neurodiversity □ Other_____

ASK YOURSELF

What made me pick up this book? _____

_____

_____

_____

_____

Did it deliver? How so? _____

_____

_____

Would I recommend this book? Why or Why not? _____

_____

_____

If so, to whom? _____

_____

What was the best quote or idea I got from this book? _____

_____

_____

_____

_____

If someone challenged this book, what reason do I *think* they would give? _____

_____

_____

_____

Has it been challenged? If so, was it banned, and for what reason? _____

_____

_____

_____

_____

What would I say to people who want to ban this book? _____

_____

_____

_____

_____

_____

My Outlaw Library: Book #5
READS IN PROTEST

BOOK_____

AUTHOR_____

GENRE_____ DATE FINISHED_____

RATE THE FOLLOWING (1–10):

Characters _____ Plot/Narrative _____ Illustrations (if applicable) _____

HOW I READ IT   □ Print   □ Audiobook   □ eBook

WHERE I GOT IT   □ Bookstore   □ Library   □ Friend   □ Other

MOODS/VIBES

1._____

2._____

3._____

4._____

5._____

REPRESENTATION

□ BIPOC □ LGBTQIA+ □ Immigrant □ Disability □ Neurodiversity □ Other_____

ASK YOURSELF

What made me pick up this book? _____

_____

_____

_____

_____

Did it deliver? How so? _____

_____

Would I recommend this book? Why or Why not? _____

_____

If so, to whom? _____

What was the best quote or idea I got from this book? _____

_____

_____

_____

_____

If someone challenged this book, what reason do I *think* they would give? _____

_____

_____

_____

Has it been challenged? If so, was it banned, and for what reason? _____

_____

_____

_____

_____

What would I say to people who want to ban this book? _____

_____

_____

_____

_____

_____

My Outlaw Library: Book #6

"Censorship feeds the dirty mind more than the four-letter word itself would."

—Dick Cavett, American talk show host and entertainer (1936–)

BOOK _____

AUTHOR _____

GENRE _____ DATE FINISHED _____

RATE THE FOLLOWING (1–10):

Characters _____ Plot/Narrative _____ Illustrations (if applicable) _____

HOW I READ IT ☐ Print ☐ Audiobook ☐ eBook

WHERE I GOT IT ☐ Bookstore ☐ Library ☐ Friend ☐ Other

MOODS/VIBES

1. _____

2. _____

3. _____

4. _____

5. _____

REPRESENTATION

☐ BIPOC ☐ LGBTQIA+ ☐ Immigrant ☐ Disability ☐ Neurodiversity ☐ Other_____

ASK YOURSELF

What made me pick up this book? _____

_____

_____

_____

_____

Did it deliver? How so? _____

_____

_____

Would I recommend this book? Why or Why not? _____

_____

_____

If so, to whom? _____

_____

What was the best quote or idea I got from this book? _____

_____

_____

_____

_____

If someone challenged this book, what reason do I *think* they would give? _____

_____

_____

_____

Has it been challenged? If so, was it banned, and for what reason? _____

_____

_____

_____

_____

What would I say to people who want to ban this book? _____

_____

_____

_____

_____

_____

My Outlaw Library: Book #7

Don't let this book become a substitute for firewood at right-wing events.

BOOK _____

AUTHOR _____

GENRE _____ DATE FINISHED _____

RATE THE FOLLOWING (1–10):

Characters _____ Plot/Narrative _____ Illustrations (if applicable) _____

HOW I READ IT ☐ Print ☐ Audiobook ☐ eBook

WHERE I GOT IT ☐ Bookstore ☐ Library ☐ Friend ☐ Other

MOODS/VIBES

1. _____

2. _____

3. _____

4. _____

5. _____

REPRESENTATION

☐ BIPOC ☐ LGBTQIA+ ☐ Immigrant ☐ Disability ☐ Neurodiversity ☐ Other_____

ASK YOURSELF

What made me pick up this book? _____

_____

_____

_____

_____

Did it deliver? How so? _____

_____

_____

Would I recommend this book? Why or Why not? _____

_____

_____

If so, to whom? _____

_____

What was the best quote or idea I got from this book? _____

_____

_____

_____

_____

_____

If someone challenged this book, what reason do I *think* they would give? _____

_____

_____

_____

_____

Has it been challenged? If so, was it banned, and for what reason? _____

_____

_____

_____

_____

What would I say to people who want to ban this book? _____

_____

_____

_____

_____

_____

Because They Don't Want You To (PART 2)

Whether they were banned for their inclusion of the marginalized, the questioning of authority or a half-baked combination of the two, the books that follow—along with those on pgs. 30–31, 62–63 and 74–75—deserve a place in our culture.

THE MATT KRAUSE BOOK LIST

IN 2021, NOW-FORMER Texas congressman Matt Krause compiled a list of 850 books that he sent to schools, asking them to confirm whether or not they had them on the shelves. This list targeted books that discuss sexuality, racism and U.S. history among other topics.

☐ **ANA ON THE EDGE** *by A.J. Sass*
This is a beautiful middle-grade story about a young ice skater named Ana exploring their gender identity. When Ana's new friend Hayden mistakes them for a boy, they go with it. Because this book deals with topics of gender identity and features trans representation, it is frequently banned or challenged.

☐ **THE BREAKAWAYS** *by Cathy G. Johnson*
This is a graphic novel for all of us forced to play team sports—especially those who definitely should not be playing team sports. The diverse group of kids on this middle school soccer team are weird, funny and struggling with their own issues. As you have probably guessed, it's this diversity that gets the book banned, along with sexual themes.

☐ **WAIT, WHAT?: A COMIC BOOK GUIDE TO RELATIONSHIPS, BODIES, AND GROWING UP** *by Heather Corinna*
This graphic nonfiction book is accessible, affirming and inclusive across all types of gender identities, sexualities and body types. It contains accurate information related to sex, puberty and (most importantly) consent! I wish there were books like this when I was a teenager.

☐ **PRINCE & KNIGHT** *by Daniel Haack, illustrated by Stevie Lewis*
Everyone deserves to see themselves in a fairy tale! And this adorable story of a prince who sets out to save his kingdom from a dragon and and falls for a good old-fashioned knight in shining armor is a fairy tale many LGBTQIA+ folks wish was around when they were younger. It's simple and sweet in the best way. And, because it depicts two men in love, it makes people angry.

☐ **MY RAINBOW** *by Trinity and DeShanna Neal*
I am in love with this picture book. It is vibrant and loving and does a great job of pushing back on gender norms for both cis and trans women! Plus, it has neurodivergent representation as well!

MOST POPULAR OVERALL BANS

OFTENTIMES, THE TRENDS for banned books match the trends in pop culture. Here are some banned books that were big hits at the time.

☐ **TWILIGHT** *by Stephanie Meyer*
Meyer's series first hit the top 10 list in 2009, right as the *Twilight* phenomenon hit its peak. Challengers claimed that it was sexually explicit, unsuitable for the age group, and had a "religious viewpoint" (specifically, occultism).

☐ **FIFTY SHADES OF GREY** *by E.L. James*
First published in 2011, this series scorched the bestseller list and hit the top 10 banned list in 2012. Various challenges cited it as being sexually explicit, unsuitable for the age group, having offensive language and more (including my favorite, "poorly written"!).

☐ **THE HUNGER GAMES** *by Suzanne Collins*
The bestselling dystopian YA series first hit the top 10 banned books list in 2010 and

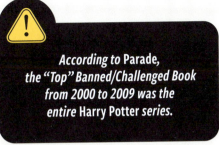

According to **Parade**, the *"Top" Banned/Challenged Book* from *2000 to 2009* was the entire **Harry Potter** *series.*

has graced the list three separate times. Challengers claim the books are occult/satanic, anti-family, violent, sexually explicit and unsuitable for the age group.

☐ **HARRY POTTER** *by J.K. Rowling*
The *Harry Potter* series is an interesting look at how challenges shift over time. In the early 2000s, Harry's saga topped the most banned and challenged books list multiple times due to occult and satanic fears. But as we've entered the 2020s, the books are now being objected to because the characters are rife with harmful stereotypes and due to the anti-trans opinions of the author.

☐ **THIRTEEN REASONS WHY** *by Jay Asher*
Published in 2007, this book was no stranger to being challenged even before it was an on-screen phenomenon. But when the Netflix adaptation was released in 2017, *Thirteen Reasons Why* saw a resurgence in bans and challenges! It actually topped that year's list of most banned or challenged books for its depiction of suicide.

97 books challenged at once in October 2022 in Beaufort, South Carolina, were immediately pulled from access, pending review. At the time of publication, they were still removed.

There are worse crimes than burning books. One of them is not reading them.

Joseph Brodsky

The books that the world calls immoral are books that show its own shame.

Oscar Wilde, *The Picture of Dorian Gray*

My Outlaw Library: Book #8
Conservatives obviously have no taste because this book is amazing.

BOOK_____

AUTHOR_____

GENRE_____ DATE FINISHED_____

RATE THE FOLLOWING (1–10):

Characters _____ Plot/Narrative _____ Illustrations (if applicable) _____

HOW I READ IT □ Print □ Audiobook □ eBook

WHERE I GOT IT □ Bookstore □ Library □ Friend □ Other

MOODS/VIBES

1._____

2._____

3._____

4._____

5._____

REPRESENTATION

□ BIPOC □ LGBTQIA+ □ Immigrant □ Disability □ Neurodiversity □ Other_____

ASK YOURSELF

What made me pick up this book? _____

_____

_____

_____

_____

Did it deliver? How so? _____

_____

_____

Would I recommend this book? Why or Why not? _____

_____

_____

If so, to whom? _____

_____

What was the best quote or idea I got from this book? _____

_____

_____

_____

_____

If someone challenged this book, what reason do I *think* they would give? ___

_____

_____

_____

Has it been challenged? If so, was it banned, and for what reason? _____

_____

_____

_____

_____

What would I say to people who want to ban this book? _____

_____

_____

_____

_____

_____

My Outlaw Library: Book #9
I came, I saw, I let go of my insular perspective.

BOOK _____

AUTHOR _____

GENRE _____ DATE FINISHED _____

RATE THE FOLLOWING (1–10):

Characters _____ Plot/Narrative _____ Illustrations (if applicable) _____

HOW I READ IT ☐ Print ☐ Audiobook ☐ eBook

WHERE I GOT IT ☐ Bookstore ☐ Library ☐ Friend ☐ Other

MOODS/VIBES

1. _____
2. _____
3. _____
4. _____
5. _____

REPRESENTATION

☐ BIPOC ☐ LGBTQIA+ ☐ Immigrant ☐ Disability ☐ Neurodiversity ☐ Other_____

ASK YOURSELF

What made me pick up this book? _____

_____

_____

_____

_____

Did it deliver? How so? _____

_____

_____

Would I recommend this book? Why or Why not? _____

_____

_____

If so, to whom? _____

_____

What was the best quote or idea I got from this book? _____

_____

_____

_____

_____

If someone challenged this book, what reason do I *think* they would give? _____

_____

_____

_____

_____

Has it been challenged? If so, was it banned, and for what reason? _____

_____

_____

_____

_____

_____

What would I say to people who want to ban this book? _____

_____

_____

_____

_____

_____

_____

My Outlaw Library: Book #10

"Never do anything against conscience even if the state demands it."
—Albert Einstein (1879–1955)

BOOK_____

AUTHOR_____

GENRE_____ DATE FINISHED_____

RATE THE FOLLOWING (1–10):

Characters _____ Plot/Narrative _____ Illustrations (if applicable) _____

HOW I READ IT ☐ Print   ☐ Audiobook   ☐ eBook

WHERE I GOT IT ☐ Bookstore   ☐ Library   ☐ Friend   ☐ Other

MOODS/VIBES

1._____

2._____

3._____

4._____

5._____

REPRESENTATION

☐ BIPOC ☐ LGBTQIA+ ☐ Immigrant ☐ Disability ☐ Neurodiversity ☐ Other_____

ASK YOURSELF

What made me pick up this book? _____

_____

_____

_____

_____

Did it deliver? How so? _____

_____

_____

Would I recommend this book? Why or Why not? _____

_____

_____

If so, to whom? _____

_____

What was the best quote or idea I got from this book? _____

_____

_____

_____

_____

If someone challenged this book, what reason do I *think* they would give? _____

_____

_____

_____

Has it been challenged? If so, was it banned, and for what reason? _____

_____

_____

_____

_____

What would I say to people who want to ban this book? _____

_____

_____

_____

_____

_____

_____

My Outlaw Library: Book #11
This machine kills harmful stereotypes.

BOOK_____

AUTHOR_____

GENRE_____ DATE FINISHED_____

RATE THE FOLLOWING (1–10):

Characters _____ Plot/Narrative _____ Illustrations (if applicable) _____

HOW I READ IT ☐ Print ☐ Audiobook ☐ eBook

WHERE I GOT IT ☐ Bookstore ☐ Library ☐ Friend ☐ Other

MOODS/VIBES

1._____

2._____

3._____

4._____

5._____

REPRESENTATION

☐ BIPOC ☐ LGBTQIA+ ☐ Immigrant ☐ Disability ☐ Neurodiversity ☐ Other_____

ASK YOURSELF

What made me pick up this book? _____

_____

_____

_____

_____

Did it deliver? How so? _____

_____

_____

Would I recommend this book? Why or Why not? _____

_____

_____

If so, to whom? _____

_____

What was the best quote or idea I got from this book? _____

_____

_____

_____

_____

If someone challenged this book, what reason do I *think* they would give? _____

_____

_____

_____

Has it been challenged? If so, was it banned, and for what reason? _____

_____

_____

_____

_____

What would I say to people who want to ban this book? _____

_____

_____

_____

_____

_____

My Outlaw Library: Book #12

There is nothing more dangerous to the censor than an open mind.

BOOK_____

AUTHOR_____

GENRE_____ DATE FINISHED_____

RATE THE FOLLOWING (1–10):

Characters _____ Plot/Narrative _____ Illustrations (if applicable) _____

HOW I READ IT □ Print □ Audiobook □ eBook

WHERE I GOT IT □ Bookstore □ Library □ Friend □ Other

MOODS/VIBES

1._____

2._____

3._____

4._____

5._____

REPRESENTATION

□ BIPOC □ LGBTQIA+ □ Immigrant □ Disability □ Neurodiversity □ Other_____

ASK YOURSELF

What made me pick up this book? _____

_____

_____

_____

_____

Did it deliver? How so? _____

_____

_____

Would I recommend this book? Why or Why not? _____

_____

_____

If so, to whom? _____

_____

What was the best quote or idea I got from this book? _____

_____

_____

_____

_____

_____

If someone challenged this book, what reason do I *think* they would give? _____

_____

_____

_____

_____

Has it been challenged? If so, was it banned, and for what reason? _____

_____

_____

_____

_____

_____

What would I say to people who want to ban this book? _____

_____

_____

_____

_____

_____

_____

My Outlaw Library: Book #13

There's a reason we call the historical period when no one could read "the Dark Ages."

BOOK_____

AUTHOR_____

GENRE_____ **DATE FINISHED**_____

RATE THE FOLLOWING (1–10):

Characters _____ Plot/Narrative _____ Illustrations (if applicable) _____

HOW I READ IT □ Print □ Audiobook □ eBook

WHERE I GOT IT □ Bookstore □ Library □ Friend □ Other

MOODS/VIBES

1._____

2._____

3._____

4._____

5._____

REPRESENTATION

□ BIPOC □ LGBTQIA+ □ Immigrant □ Disability □ Neurodiversity □ Other_____

ASK YOURSELF

What made me pick up this book? _____

_____

_____

_____

_____

Did it deliver? How so? _____

_____

_____

Would I recommend this book? Why or Why not? _____

_____

_____

If so, to whom? _____

_____

What was the best quote or idea I got from this book? _____

_____

_____

_____

_____

If someone challenged this book, what reason do I *think* they would give? _____

_____

_____

_____

_____

Has it been challenged? If so, was it banned, and for what reason? _____

_____

_____

_____

_____

What would I say to people who want to ban this book? _____

_____

_____

_____

_____

_____

_____

My Outlaw Library: Book #14

Books: Because glasses aren't the only things that help you see with greater clarity.

BOOK_____

AUTHOR_____

GENRE_____ DATE FINISHED_____

RATE THE FOLLOWING (1–10):

Characters _____ Plot/Narrative _____ Illustrations (if applicable) _____

HOW I READ IT ☐ Print ☐ Audiobook ☐ eBook

WHERE I GOT IT ☐ Bookstore ☐ Library ☐ Friend ☐ Other

MOODS/VIBES

1._____

2._____

3._____

4._____

5._____

REPRESENTATION

☐ BIPOC ☐ LGBTQIA+ ☐ Immigrant ☐ Disability ☐ Neurodiversity ☐ Other_____

ASK YOURSELF

What made me pick up this book? _____

_____

_____

_____

_____

Did it deliver? How so? _____

_____

_____

Would I recommend this book? Why or Why not? _____

_____

_____

If so, to whom? _____

_____

What was the best quote or idea I got from this book? _____

_____

_____

_____

_____

_____

If someone challenged this book, what reason do I *think* they would give? _____

_____

_____

_____

_____

Has it been challenged? If so, was it banned, and for what reason? _____

_____

_____

_____

_____

_____

What would I say to people who want to ban this book? _____

_____

_____

_____

_____

_____

My Outlaw Library: Book #15
Build a library that would make
Moms for Liberty froth at the mouth.

BOOK_____

AUTHOR_____

GENRE_____ DATE FINISHED_____

RATE THE FOLLOWING (1–10):

Characters _____ Plot/Narrative _____ Illustrations (if applicable) _____

HOW I READ IT ☐ Print ☐ Audiobook ☐ eBook

WHERE I GOT IT ☐ Bookstore ☐ Library ☐ Friend ☐ Other

MOODS/VIBES

1._____
2._____
3._____
4._____
5._____

REPRESENTATION

☐ BIPOC ☐ LGBTQIA+ ☐ Immigrant ☐ Disability ☐ Neurodiversity ☐ Other_____

ASK YOURSELF

What made me pick up this book? _____
_____
_____
_____
_____

Did it deliver? How so? _____

_____

Would I recommend this book? Why or Why not? _____

_____

_____

If so, to whom? _____

What was the best quote or idea I got from this book? _____

_____

_____

_____

_____

If someone challenged this book, what reason do I *think* they would give? ____

_____

_____

_____

Has it been challenged? If so, was it banned, and for what reason? _____

_____

_____

_____

_____

What would I say to people who want to ban this book? _____

_____

_____

_____

_____

_____

Because They Don't Want You To (PART 3)

Whether they were banned for their inclusion of the marginalized, the questioning of authority or a half-baked combination of the two, the books that follow—along with those on pgs. 30–31, 42–43 and 74–75— deserve a place in our culture.

LGBTQIA+ PICTURE BOOKS

I GENUINELY BELIEVE great books know no age limit. Picture books do an incredible job of conveying big emotions, ideas and stories in ways that are easier to grasp, and can be relatable for all ages!

□ AND TANGO MAKES THREE
by Justin Richardson and Peter Parnell
This book is too cute for words and makes an excellent baby shower or birthday present especially when paired with a penguin stuffie! It tells the true story of two male chinstrap penguins at the Central Park Zoo who together raised a baby penguin named Tango. Regularly featured in the annual top 10 list for being anti-family and promoting the gay agenda.

□ THIS DAY IN JUNE *by Gayle Pittman, illustrated by Krystyna Litten*
Bright, bold, fun and engaging, it's everything you want in a picture book.

It celebrates LGBTQIA+ pride without judgment or reservation, which is exactly why it is so frequently banned and challenged. Claims that it is promoting homosexuality, indoctrinating kids and is inappropriate overall are regularly used in challenges.

□ MY SHADOW IS PINK *by Scott Stuart*
This is one of the most beautiful books I have ever read! Written after an experience with his son wanting to dress up as Elsa, Scott's story about a boy whose shadow doesn't match what culture says it should is a powerful story of love and affirmation. I cry every time I read it. But it is regularly banned and challenged for being divisive and promoting alternative gender ideologies.

□ I AM JAZZ *by Jessica Herthel and Jazz Jennings*
Published in 2014, this autobiographical picture book has been on most banned lists regularly. Jazz wanted to write a book sharing her real-life experiences

as a transgender child, and this kind of representation is absolutely vital for kids. However, that is the very same reason why it is frequently banned or challenged.

☐ CALL ME MAX *by Kyle Lukoff*

This is a story about identity, but really it is a story of kindness and the simplicity of respecting others. Max starts school and shares his feelings about his identity with new friends and his parents. It's a beautiful introduction to helping kids understand the trans experience, which is the primary reason it's been so frequently challenged.

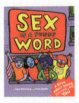

SEX ED

THIS HAS ALWAYS been a topic prone to bans and challenges in the United States. Books that talk about sex, sexual identity, birth control or other issues are viewed as pornographic or believed to encourage kids to have sex. But the reality is that these books keep kids safe by giving them the language to understand incredibly personal topics like consent, safety and self-advocacy.

☐ SEX IS A FUNNY WORD

by Cory Silverberg and Fiona Smyth
I love that this book is designed to facilitate conversations between kids (8–10 years old) and their adults. It asks questions, gives discussion prompts and is designed to be interactive in a way that makes it a little bit uncomfortable for those of us who were

never allowed to have frank conversations about this topic as kids. It's frequently challenged and banned for references to gender identity and sex education and for its "inappropriate" illustrations.

☐ YOU KNOW, SEX *by Cory Silverberg and Fiona Smyth*

This one is for kids 10+ and is a great follow-up to *Sex Is a Funny Word*, with more of a focus on intimacy and sex (vs. the puberty-driven focus of *Sex Is a Funny Word*). It gets banned or challenged for all the same reasons as the authors' other book.

☐ S.E.X. *by Heather Corinna*

This is my go-to recommendation for teens and young adults who have questions about sex, sexuality, gender and more. Written in a fully inclusive and non-judgmental manner, this book covers EVERYTHING you need to know, and then some. The very same things I love about this book are (surprise) the exact reasons that it gets challenged.

☐ IT'S PERFECTLY NORMAL *by Robie Harris, illustrated by Michael Emberley*

Since its initial publishing in 1994, this book has been frequently challenged or banned because opponents allege it has inappropriate illustrations and pornographic content. Written for kids 10+, it is a staple of sex education because it is written with safety and accuracy in mind. The latest edition has been updated to include timely information, covering internet safety, STIs and more.

Between July and September 2022, the last time period for which there is complete data, 56 percent of bans targeted YA titles.

There are no bad authors for children...because every child is different. They can find the stories they need to, and they bring themselves to stories.

Neil Gaiman

Any book worth banning is a book worth reading.

Isaac Asimov

My Outlaw Library: Book #16

"I dislike censorship. Like the appendix it is useless when inert and dangerous when active."
—Gerald Maurice Edelman, American biochemist and Nobel prize winner in medicine (1929–2014)

BOOK _____

AUTHOR _____

GENRE _____ DATE FINISHED _____

RATE THE FOLLOWING (1–10):

Characters _____ Plot/Narrative _____ Illustrations (if applicable) _____

HOW I READ IT   ☐ Print   ☐ Audiobook   ☐ eBook

WHERE I GOT IT   ☐ Bookstore   ☐ Library   ☐ Friend   ☐ Other

MOODS/VIBES

1. _____

2. _____

3. _____

4. _____

5. _____

REPRESENTATION

☐ BIPOC ☐ LGBTQIA+ ☐ Immigrant ☐ Disability ☐ Neurodiversity ☐ Other_____

ASK YOURSELF

What made me pick up this book? _____

_____

_____

_____

_____

Did it deliver? How so? _____

_____

_____

Would I recommend this book? Why or Why not? _____

_____

_____

If so, to whom? _____

_____

What was the best quote or idea I got from this book? _____

_____

_____

_____

_____

_____

If someone challenged this book, what reason do I *think* they would give? _____

_____

_____

_____

_____

Has it been challenged? If so, was it banned, and for what reason? _____

_____

_____

_____

_____

_____

What would I say to people who want to ban this book? _____

_____

_____

_____

_____

_____

_____

My Outlaw Library: Book #17

Breaking the cycle of intergenerational trauma, one page at a time.

BOOK _____

AUTHOR _____

GENRE _____ DATE FINISHED _____

RATE THE FOLLOWING (1–10):

Characters _____ Plot/Narrative _____ Illustrations (if applicable) _____

HOW I READ IT □ Print □ Audiobook □ eBook

WHERE I GOT IT □ Bookstore □ Library □ Friend □ Other

MOODS/VIBES

1. _____
2. _____
3. _____
4. _____
5. _____

REPRESENTATION

□ BIPOC □ LGBTQIA+ □ Immigrant □ Disability □ Neurodiversity □ Other _____

ASK YOURSELF

What made me pick up this book? _____

_____

_____

_____

_____

Did it deliver? How so? _____
_____
_____

Would I recommend this book? Why or Why not? _____
_____
_____

If so, to whom? _____
_____

What was the best quote or idea I got from this book? _____
_____
_____
_____
_____
_____

If someone challenged this book, what reason do I *think* they would give? _____
_____
_____
_____
_____

Has it been challenged? If so, was it banned, and for what reason? _____
_____
_____
_____
_____
_____

What would I say to people who want to ban this book? _____
_____
_____
_____
_____
_____
_____

My Outlaw Library: Book #18
This book isn't very popular with the tiki torch crowd. All the more reason to read it.

BOOK_____

AUTHOR_____

GENRE_____ DATE FINISHED_____

RATE THE FOLLOWING (1–10):

Characters _____ Plot/Narrative _____ Illustrations (if applicable) _____

HOW I READ IT ☐ Print ☐ Audiobook ☐ eBook

WHERE I GOT IT ☐ Bookstore ☐ Library ☐ Friend ☐ Other

MOODS/VIBES

1._____

2._____

3._____

4._____

5._____

REPRESENTATION

☐ BIPOC ☐ LGBTQIA+ ☐ Immigrant ☐ Disability ☐ Neurodiversity ☐ Other_____

ASK YOURSELF

What made me pick up this book? _____

_____

_____

_____

_____

Did it deliver? How so? _____

_____

_____

Would I recommend this book? Why or Why not? _____

_____

_____

If so, to whom? _____

What was the best quote or idea I got from this book? _____

_____

_____

_____

_____

If someone challenged this book, what reason do I *think* they would give? _____

_____

_____

_____

Has it been challenged? If so, was it banned, and for what reason? _____

_____

_____

_____

_____

What would I say to people who want to ban this book? _____

_____

_____

_____

_____

_____

_____

Voices of the People
Question 2: Dialogue

In my interviews with real folks impacted by book challenges,
I found fright, outrage and anger, but also a bit of hope (thanks, students!)
In Part 2, we discuss the following question:

What is something you wish book banners could understand?

I wish that they understood the harm they're doing when they challenge and ban books. I wish they knew how isolated and lost and hurt they're making so many people feel. They're not protecting children (or anyone else) by taking these books away.

—Emily Lessig,
The Violet Fox Bookshop, Virginia

They're not protecting kids with this: That's a fundamentally dishonest point of view, given that we know things like representation and acceptance of queer children is known to prevent suicide and keep kids happier and healthier. THAT is protecting children, not this ridiculous insistence that kids are too young to learn what a pronoun is.

—Anna, Teacher

School libraries do not have pornography. Period. It isn't there and if they want to make sure that their students have access to relevant materials in their school then they need to advocate for certified school library staff whose job it is to make sure that students get access to resources and work with parents to help their individual student.

—Anonymous School Librarian

Your beliefs guide YOU and your family: Not [me and] mine.

—Holly C., Parent

[The right] are trying to ban the civil right that permits them to challenge a title. It is like standing on a branch and sawing it off at the trunk of the tree behind you.

—Lance Werner, Librarian

At the end of the day, it's just a book. There's no reason to get upset over the fact that something you don't support was included in a book you don't even have to read. It's not hurting anybody. Just don't read the book! It's that simple! Let other people enjoy it. It's the least you could do.

—Ainslee Flanagan, Student

Empathy. Also, logic.

—Jeff, Teacher

Because They Don't Want You To (PART 4)

Whether they were banned for their inclusion of the marginalized, the questioning of authority or a half-baked combination of the two, the books that follow—along with those on pgs. 30–31, 42–43, 62–63— deserve a place in our culture.

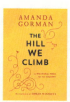

ANTI-RACIST BOOKS

IT IS UNFORTUNATELY very easy to understand why 2020 was a particularly interesting year for book challenges. Many schools and libraries were closed due to the pandemic, so the total number of challenges was down. But it was the content of those challenges that really changed. Following the protests that occurred after the killing of George Floyd, books related to police violence, racism and anti-racism all had an uptick in challenges.

☐ **SOMETHING HAPPENED IN OUR TOWN: A CHILD'S STORY ABOUT RACIAL INJUSTICE** *by Marianne Celano, Marietta Collins and Ann Hazzard, illustrated by Jennifer Zivoin*
This is one of those books you wish didn't need to exist. But it does, so we should be glad it's available. Written by three psychologists, this book helps adults talk with kids about racial injustice and violence. It has been challenged and banned for divisive language and promoting anti-police views.

☐ **STAMPED: RACISM, ANTI-RACISM, AND YOU** *by Jason Reynolds and Ibram X. Kendi*
This YA adaptation of Dr. Kendi's book *Stamped from The Beginning* is one of my favorite YA adaptations ever! Jason Reynolds is a fiction writer, and he uses a very engaging style that I recommend for readers of all ages. It's regularly challenged and banned due to claims that it engages in "selective storytelling" and does not include racism against all people. Sometimes it's challenged because some people simply do not like Kendi.

☐ **ALL BOYS AREN'T BLUE**
by George M. Johnson
This book lives at the intersection of queer life and Black life in the U.S. And because it covers the two most common topics that are banned or challenged, it's no surprise that it has been on the top 10 list multiple times. This is a book everyone should read, regardless of their backgrounds, because it speaks to the universal feeling of being out of place and alone.

☐ THE HILL WE CLIMB
by Amanda Gorman

Like many, I was transfixed as I watched former youth poet laureate Amanda Gorman recite her poem "The Hill We Climb" at the 2021 U.S. presidential inauguration. The print version of this poem was challenged at a Florida school for indirect hate speech and lacking educational content.

☐ NEW KID
by Jerry Craft

I love this graphic novel so much. It's fun and funny and perfectly highlights the awkwardness of middle school. But references to microaggressions and other racist actions are enough for it to be regularly challenged and banned, with objectors often citing the alleged promotion of CRT (critical race theory) and racism.

ADD YOUR OWN ENTRIES

Which other books under scrutiny need to be stood up for?

TITLE: _____

AUTHOR: _____

TITLE: _____

AUTHOR: _____

TITLE: _____

AUTHOR: _____

TITLE: _____

AUTHOR: _____

TITLE: _____

AUTHOR: _____

TITLE: _____

AUTHOR: _____

TITLE: _____

AUTHOR: _____

Definitions belong to the definers— not the defined.

Toni Morrison, *Beloved*

A book is a version of the world. If you do not like it, ignore it; or offer your own version in return.

Salman Rushdie, "*In Good Faith***"**

So You Want to Read a Banned Book

What happens when a book is banned in your community? How do you access one if you can't find it locally? Start here.

IN STORES

As of right now, it is not illegal to own or read books that have been banned. But that doesn't stop some people from trying to make reading a crime. Lawmakers in Virginia sued to stop Barnes & Noble from selling *Gender Queer* and *A Court of Mist and Fury* without parental permission.

While that particular effort failed, there are attempts across the country to ban the sale of "explicit" books to schools, teachers or minors. A recent law in Texas would require booksellers to issue ratings for all books sold that might end up in a classroom. It's currently being fought in court.

If you have the means to purchase a book, you can do so by supporting your favorite indie bookstore or online through websites like *bookshop.org*, but buying books isn't always financially viable—especially for young people.

PUBLIC LIBRARIES

If a book has been banned in your area, check with your local library to see if they have it. If not, request it. If you live in a larger town with more than one library, you might find a book that's been banned in one on the shelves at another.

Some libraries offer access to their digital collections to students free of charge. The Brooklyn Public Library's Books Unbanned initiative offers a free BPL eCard for anyone ages 13 to 21, allowing them to access the library's full ebook and elearning collection—a tremendous resource for students everywhere.

Another resource is the Digital Public Library of America, which allows free access to ebook versions of banned books based on your location via an app. This is also a fantastic way to learn what books have been banned or challenged near you.

COLLEGE AND UNIVERSITY LIBRARIES

Most of the legislation targeted at school and public libraries is limited to K–12, which means your local college campus might have a book the public library was forced to pull from shelves. Many campuses will extend access to members of the larger community.

To gain access, first check to see if your library is a part of an interlibrary loan system. This allows you to check out books from libraries across your geographic area (including those on college campuses) and have them delivered to your local library to pick up.

My Outlaw Library: Book #19

Books: Amplifying marginalized voices without ever saying a word.

BOOK_____

AUTHOR_____

GENRE_____ DATE FINISHED_____

RATE THE FOLLOWING (1–10):

Characters _____ Plot/Narrative _____ Illustrations (if applicable) _____

HOW I READ IT   ☐ Print   ☐ Audiobook   ☐ eBook

WHERE I GOT IT   ☐ Bookstore   ☐ Library   ☐ Friend   ☐ Other

MOODS/VIBES

1._____
2._____
3._____
4._____
5._____

REPRESENTATION

☐ BIPOC ☐ LGBTQIA+ ☐ Immigrant ☐ Disability ☐ Neurodiversity ☐ Other_____

ASK YOURSELF

What made me pick up this book? _____
_____
_____
_____
_____

Did it deliver? How so? _____

_____

_____

Would I recommend this book? Why or Why not? _____

_____

_____

If so, to whom? _____

_____

What was the best quote or idea I got from this book? _____

_____

_____

_____

_____

_____

If someone challenged this book, what reason do I *think* they would give? _____

_____

_____

_____

_____

Has it been challenged? If so, was it banned, and for what reason? _____

_____

_____

_____

_____

_____

What would I say to people who want to ban this book? _____

_____

_____

_____

_____

_____

My Outlaw Library: Book #20

"Censure acquits the raven, but pursues the dove."
—Juvenal, Roman poet (1st century–2nd century C.E.)

BOOK _____

AUTHOR _____

GENRE _____ DATE FINISHED _____

RATE THE FOLLOWING (1–10):

Characters _____ Plot/Narrative _____ Illustrations (if applicable) _____

HOW I READ IT ☐ Print ☐ Audiobook ☐ eBook

WHERE I GOT IT ☐ Bookstore ☐ Library ☐ Friend ☐ Other

MOODS/VIBES

1. _____

2. _____

3. _____

4. _____

5. _____

REPRESENTATION

☐ BIPOC ☐ LGBTQIA+ ☐ Immigrant ☐ Disability ☐ Neurodiversity ☐ Other_____

ASK YOURSELF

What made me pick up this book? _____

_____

_____

_____

_____

Did it deliver? How so? _____

_____

_____

Would I recommend this book? Why or Why not? _____

_____

_____

If so, to whom? _____

_____

What was the best quote or idea I got from this book? _____

_____

_____

_____

_____

If someone challenged this book, what reason do I *think* they would give? _____

_____

_____

_____

Has it been challenged? If so, was it banned, and for what reason? _____

_____

_____

_____

_____

What would I say to people who want to ban this book? _____

_____

_____

_____

_____

_____

My Outlaw Library: Book #21
Trees gave their lives so these ideas could piss off bigots.

BOOK_____

AUTHOR_____

GENRE_____ DATE FINISHED_____

RATE THE FOLLOWING (1–10):

Characters _____ Plot/Narrative _____ Illustrations (if applicable) _____

HOW I READ IT □ Print   □ Audiobook   □ eBook

WHERE I GOT IT □ Bookstore   □ Library   □ Friend   □ Other

MOODS/VIBES

1._____
2._____
3._____
4._____
5._____

REPRESENTATION

□ BIPOC □ LGBTQIA+ □ Immigrant □ Disability □ Neurodiversity □ Other_____

ASK YOURSELF

What made me pick up this book? _____
_____
_____
_____
_____

Did it deliver? How so? _____

_____

_____

Would I recommend this book? Why or Why not? _____

_____

_____

If so, to whom? _____

_____

What was the best quote or idea I got from this book? _____

_____

_____

_____

_____

If someone challenged this book, what reason do I *think* they would give? _____

_____

_____

_____

_____

Has it been challenged? If so, was it banned, and for what reason? _____

_____

_____

_____

_____

_____

What would I say to people who want to ban this book? _____

_____

_____

_____

_____

_____

_____

My Outlaw Library: Book #22

See what history's victors don't want you to know.

BOOK_____

AUTHOR_____

GENRE_____ DATE FINISHED_____

RATE THE FOLLOWING (1–10):

Characters _____ Plot/Narrative _____ Illustrations (if applicable) _____

HOW I READ IT   □ Print   □ Audiobook   □ eBook

WHERE I GOT IT   □ Bookstore   □ Library   □ Friend   □ Other

MOODS/VIBES

1._____
2._____
3._____
4._____
5._____

REPRESENTATION

□ BIPOC   □ LGBTQIA+   □ Immigrant   □ Disability   □ Neurodiversity   □ Other_____

ASK YOURSELF

What made me pick up this book? _____

_____

_____

_____

_____

Did it deliver? How so? _____

_____

_____

Would I recommend this book? Why or Why not? _____

_____

_____

If so, to whom? _____

_____

What was the best quote or idea I got from this book? _____

_____

_____

_____

_____

_____

If someone challenged this book, what reason do I *think* they would give? _____

_____

_____

_____

_____

Has it been challenged? If so, was it banned, and for what reason? _____

_____

_____

_____

_____

_____

What would I say to people who want to ban this book? _____

_____

_____

_____

_____

_____

_____

My Outlaw Library: Book #23

"They can't censor the gleam in my eye."
—Charles Laughton, British actor (1899–1962)

BOOK_____

AUTHOR_____

GENRE_____ DATE FINISHED_____

RATE THE FOLLOWING (1–10):

Characters _____ Plot/Narrative _____ Illustrations (if applicable) _____

HOW I READ IT ☐ Print ☐ Audiobook ☐ eBook

WHERE I GOT IT ☐ Bookstore ☐ Library ☐ Friend ☐ Other

MOODS/VIBES

1._____
2._____
3._____
4._____
5._____

REPRESENTATION

☐ BIPOC ☐ LGBTQIA+ ☐ Immigrant ☐ Disability ☐ Neurodiversity ☐ Other_____

ASK YOURSELF

What made me pick up this book? _____
_____
_____
_____
_____

Did it deliver? How so? _____

_____

_____

Would I recommend this book? Why or Why not? _____

_____

_____

If so, to whom? _____

_____

What was the best quote or idea I got from this book? _____

_____

_____

_____

_____

_____

If someone challenged this book, what reason do I *think* they would give? _____

_____

_____

_____

Has it been challenged? If so, was it banned, and for what reason? _____

_____

_____

_____

_____

What would I say to people who want to ban this book? _____

_____

_____

_____

_____

_____

A dangerous book will
always be in danger
from those it threatens
with the demand that they
question their assumptions.
They'd rather hang on
to the assumptions and
ban the book.

Ursula K. Le Guin, "Unquestioned Assumptions"

Give me knowledge
or give me death.

Kurt Vonnegut

My Outlaw Library: Book #24
What do you mean, "Women exist outside the male gaze"?

BOOK_____

AUTHOR_____

GENRE_____ DATE FINISHED_____

RATE THE FOLLOWING (1–10):

Characters _____ Plot/Narrative _____ Illustrations (if applicable) _____

HOW I READ IT ☐ Print ☐ Audiobook ☐ eBook

WHERE I GOT IT ☐ Bookstore ☐ Library ☐ Friend ☐ Other

MOODS/VIBES

1._____
2._____
3._____
4._____
5._____

REPRESENTATION

☐ BIPOC ☐ LGBTQIA+ ☐ Immigrant ☐ Disability ☐ Neurodiversity ☐ Other_____

ASK YOURSELF

What made me pick up this book? _____

_____

_____

_____

_____

Did it deliver? How so? _____

_____

_____

Would I recommend this book? Why or Why not? _____

_____

_____

If so, to whom? _____

_____

What was the best quote or idea I got from this book? _____

_____

_____

_____

_____

_____

If someone challenged this book, what reason do I *think* they would give? _____

_____

_____

_____

_____

Has it been challenged? If so, was it banned, and for what reason? _____

_____

_____

_____

_____

_____

What would I say to people who want to ban this book? _____

_____

_____

_____

_____

_____

_____

My Outlaw Library: Book #25

New anxiety unlocked: Caring about those who don't have my level of privilege.

BOOK _____

AUTHOR _____

GENRE _____ DATE FINISHED _____

RATE THE FOLLOWING (1–10):

Characters _____ Plot/Narrative _____ Illustrations (if applicable) _____

HOW I READ IT ☐ Print ☐ Audiobook ☐ eBook

WHERE I GOT IT ☐ Bookstore ☐ Library ☐ Friend ☐ Other

MOODS/VIBES

1. _____
2. _____
3. _____
4. _____
5. _____

REPRESENTATION

☐ BIPOC ☐ LGBTQIA+ ☐ Immigrant ☐ Disability ☐ Neurodiversity ☐ Other_____

ASK YOURSELF

What made me pick up this book? _____

_____

_____

_____

_____

Did it deliver? How so? _____

_____

_____

Would I recommend this book? Why or Why not? _____

_____

_____

If so, to whom? _____

_____

What was the best quote or idea I got from this book? _____

_____

_____

_____

_____

If someone challenged this book, what reason do I *think* they would give? _____

_____

_____

_____

Has it been challenged? If so, was it banned, and for what reason? _____

_____

_____

_____

_____

What would I say to people who want to ban this book? _____

_____

_____

_____

_____

_____

_____

My Outlaw Library: Book #26
Power is a helluva drug.

BOOK_____

AUTHOR_____

GENRE_____ DATE FINISHED_____

RATE THE FOLLOWING (1–10):

Characters _____ Plot/Narrative _____ Illustrations (if applicable) _____

HOW I READ IT ☐ Print ☐ Audiobook ☐ eBook

WHERE I GOT IT ☐ Bookstore ☐ Library ☐ Friend ☐ Other

MOODS/VIBES

1._____

2._____

3._____

4._____

5._____

REPRESENTATION

☐ BIPOC ☐ LGBTQIA+ ☐ Immigrant ☐ Disability ☐ Neurodiversity ☐ Other_____

ASK YOURSELF

What made me pick up this book? _____

_____

_____

_____

_____

Did it deliver? How so? _____

_____

_____

Would I recommend this book? Why or Why not? _____

_____

_____

If so, to whom? _____

_____

What was the best quote or idea I got from this book? _____

_____

_____

_____

_____

_____

If someone challenged this book, what reason do I *think* they would give? _____

_____

_____

_____

_____

Has it been challenged? If so, was it banned, and for what reason? _____

_____

_____

_____

_____

_____

What would I say to people who want to ban this book? _____

_____

_____

_____

_____

_____

_____

Voices of the People
Question 3: General Outlook

In my interviews with real folks impacted by book challenges,
I found fright, outrage and anger, but also a bit of hope (thanks, students!)
In Part 3, we discuss the following question:

What is something you wish the general public understood about challenges/bans?

This is about more than just banning books. This is about controlling the flow of information in order to undermine our democracy.

—Anna, Teacher

There are so many ways that we can all fight back against books being challenged and banned and have a huge impact. Do not sit idly by and watch the bad guys win because it doesn't impact you directly or because you don't think you can make a difference. You can make a difference!

—Emily Lessig, The Violet Fox Bookshop, Virginia

Attempts to ban speech and thought inspire us to fight harder.

—Lance Werner, Librarian

Collection development is a science—books are very thoughtfully selected by experienced professionals, and their choices are non-partisan and represent the community they are a part of.

—Lisa Varga,
Virginia Library Association Executive Director

Censorship has never won or been seen as beneficial. Limiting ideas and points of view doesn't help any of us grow.

—Genna Brong, Parent

[Bans] are truly everywhere. Even people who think they live in more progressive areas should be concerned.

—Anonymous School Librarian

[Book bans have] nothing to do with protecting children, it is about people wanting to limit exposure to things they disagree with. For example, we'd be banning the Bible if there was actual concern about exposing children to things like violence, infidelity, incest, etc.

—Anonymous Parent

Don't join the book burners. Don't think you're going to conceal faults by concealing evidence that they ever existed. Don't be afraid to go in your library and read every book.

Dwight D. Eisenhower

The first condition of progress is the removal of censorship.

George Bernard Shaw,
Mrs. Warren's Profession

My Outlaw Library: Book #27

"Censorship, like charity, should begin at home; but unlike charity, it should end there."

—Clare Boothe Luce, American playwright and diplomat (1903–1987)

BOOK_____

AUTHOR_____

GENRE_____ DATE FINISHED_____

RATE THE FOLLOWING (1–10):

Characters _____ Plot/Narrative _____ Illustrations (if applicable) _____

HOW I READ IT ☐ Print ☐ Audiobook ☐ eBook

WHERE I GOT IT ☐ Bookstore ☐ Library ☐ Friend ☐ Other

MOODS/VIBES

1._____

2._____

3._____

4._____

5._____

REPRESENTATION

☐ BIPOC ☐ LGBTQIA+ ☐ Immigrant ☐ Disability ☐ Neurodiversity ☐ Other_____

ASK YOURSELF

What made me pick up this book? _____

_____

_____

_____

_____

Did it deliver? How so? _____

_____

_____

Would I recommend this book? Why or Why not? _____

_____

_____

If so, to whom? _____

_____

What was the best quote or idea I got from this book? _____

_____

_____

_____

_____

_____

If someone challenged this book, what reason do I *think* they would give? _____

_____

_____

_____

_____

Has it been challenged? If so, was it banned, and for what reason? _____

_____

_____

_____

_____

_____

What would I say to people who want to ban this book? _____

_____

_____

_____

_____

_____

_____

My Outlaw Library: Book #28
Can't we just ban ignorance instead?

BOOK_____

AUTHOR_____

GENRE_____ DATE FINISHED_____

RATE THE FOLLOWING (1–10):

Characters _____ Plot/Narrative _____ Illustrations (if applicable) _____

HOW I READ IT   ☐ Print   ☐ Audiobook   ☐ eBook

WHERE I GOT IT   ☐ Bookstore   ☐ Library   ☐ Friend   ☐ Other

MOODS/VIBES

1._____

2._____

3._____

4._____

5._____

REPRESENTATION

☐ BIPOC ☐ LGBTQIA+ ☐ Immigrant ☐ Disability ☐ Neurodiversity ☐ Other_____

ASK YOURSELF

What made me pick up this book? _____

_____

_____

_____

_____

Did it deliver? How so? _____

_____

_____

Would I recommend this book? Why or Why not? _____

_____

_____

If so, to whom? _____

_____

What was the best quote or idea I got from this book? _____

_____

_____

_____

_____

_____

If someone challenged this book, what reason do I *think* they would give? ____

_____

_____

_____

_____

Has it been challenged? If so, was it banned, and for what reason? _____

_____

_____

_____

_____

_____

What would I say to people who want to ban this book? _____

_____

_____

_____

_____

_____

_____

My Outlaw Library: Book #29

A great book contains something to offend everyone.

BOOK_____

AUTHOR_____

GENRE_____ DATE FINISHED_____

RATE THE FOLLOWING (1–10):

Characters _____ Plot/Narrative _____ Illustrations (if applicable) _____

HOW I READ IT ☐ Print ☐ Audiobook ☐ eBook

WHERE I GOT IT ☐ Bookstore ☐ Library ☐ Friend ☐ Other

MOODS/VIBES

1._____

2._____

3._____

4._____

5._____

REPRESENTATION

☐ BIPOC ☐ LGBTQIA+ ☐ Immigrant ☐ Disability ☐ Neurodiversity ☐ Other_____

ASK YOURSELF

What made me pick up this book? _____

_____

_____

_____

_____

Did it deliver? How so? _____
_____
_____

Would I recommend this book? Why or Why not? _____
_____
_____

If so, to whom? _____
_____

What was the best quote or idea I got from this book? _____
_____
_____
_____
_____
_____

If someone challenged this book, what reason do I *think* they would give? _____
_____
_____
_____
_____

Has it been challenged? If so, was it banned, and for what reason? _____
_____
_____
_____
_____
_____

What would I say to people who want to ban this book? _____
_____
_____
_____
_____
_____
_____

My Outlaw Library: Book #30

You can't ban books while whining about cancel culture.

BOOK _____

AUTHOR _____

GENRE _____ DATE FINISHED _____

RATE THE FOLLOWING (1–10):

Characters _____ Plot/Narrative _____ Illustrations (if applicable) _____

HOW I READ IT ☐ Print ☐ Audiobook ☐ eBook

WHERE I GOT IT ☐ Bookstore ☐ Library ☐ Friend ☐ Other

MOODS/VIBES

1. _____

2. _____

3. _____

4. _____

5. _____

REPRESENTATION

☐ BIPOC ☐ LGBTQIA+ ☐ Immigrant ☐ Disability ☐ Neurodiversity ☐ Other_____

ASK YOURSELF

What made me pick up this book? _____

_____

_____

_____

_____

Did it deliver? How so? _____

_____

_____

Would I recommend this book? Why or Why not? _____

_____

_____

If so, to whom? _____

_____

What was the best quote or idea I got from this book? _____

_____

_____

_____

_____

If someone challenged this book, what reason do I *think* they would give? ___

_____

_____

_____

Has it been challenged? If so, was it banned, and for what reason? _____

_____

_____

_____

_____

What would I say to people who want to ban this book? _____

_____

_____

_____

_____

_____

My Outlaw Library: Book #31
Books: Go to bed a little wiser than when you woke up.

BOOK_____

AUTHOR_____

GENRE_____ DATE FINISHED_____

RATE THE FOLLOWING (1–10):

Characters _____ Plot/Narrative _____ Illustrations (if applicable) _____

HOW I READ IT ☐ Print ☐ Audiobook ☐ eBook

WHERE I GOT IT ☐ Bookstore ☐ Library ☐ Friend ☐ Other

MOODS/VIBES

1._____

2._____

3._____

4._____

5._____

REPRESENTATION

☐ BIPOC ☐ LGBTQIA+ ☐ Immigrant ☐ Disability ☐ Neurodiversity ☐ Other_____

ASK YOURSELF

What made me pick up this book? _____

_____

_____

_____

_____

Did it deliver? How so? _____

_____

_____

Would I recommend this book? Why or Why not? _____

_____

_____

If so, to whom? _____

_____

What was the best quote or idea I got from this book? _____

_____

_____

_____

_____

_____

If someone challenged this book, what reason do I *think* they would give? _____

_____

_____

_____

_____

Has it been challenged? If so, was it banned, and for what reason? _____

_____

_____

_____

_____

_____

What would I say to people who want to ban this book? _____

_____

_____

_____

_____

_____

_____

My Outlaw Library: Book #32

"Censorship of anything...has always been and always will be the last resort of the boob and the bigot."

—Eugene O'Neill, American playwright (1888–1953)

BOOK_____

AUTHOR_____

GENRE_____ DATE FINISHED_____

RATE THE FOLLOWING (1–10):

Characters _____ Plot/Narrative _____ Illustrations (if applicable) _____

HOW I READ IT   ☐ Print   ☐ Audiobook   ☐ eBook

WHERE I GOT IT   ☐ Bookstore   ☐ Library   ☐ Friend   ☐ Other

MOODS/VIBES

1._____

2._____

3._____

4._____

5._____

REPRESENTATION

☐ BIPOC ☐ LGBTQIA+ ☐ Immigrant ☐ Disability ☐ Neurodiversity ☐ Other_____

ASK YOURSELF

What made me pick up this book? _____

_____

_____

_____

_____

Did it deliver? How so? _____

_____

_____

Would I recommend this book? Why or Why not? _____

_____

_____

If so, to whom? _____

What was the best quote or idea I got from this book? _____

_____

_____

_____

_____

_____

If someone challenged this book, what reason do I *think* they would give? _____

_____

_____

_____

Has it been challenged? If so, was it banned, and for what reason? _____

_____

_____

_____

_____

What would I say to people who want to ban this book? _____

_____

_____

_____

_____

_____

My Outlaw Library: Book #33
Book bans don't protect kids—they protect privilege.

BOOK_____

AUTHOR_____

GENRE_____ DATE FINISHED_____

RATE THE FOLLOWING (1–10):

Characters _____ Plot/Narrative _____ Illustrations (if applicable) _____

HOW I READ IT ☐ Print ☐ Audiobook ☐ eBook

WHERE I GOT IT ☐ Bookstore ☐ Library ☐ Friend ☐ Other

MOODS/VIBES

1._____

2._____

3._____

4._____

5._____

REPRESENTATION

☐ BIPOC ☐ LGBTQIA+ ☐ Immigrant ☐ Disability ☐ Neurodiversity ☐ Other_____

ASK YOURSELF

What made me pick up this book? _____

_____

_____

_____

_____

Did it deliver? How so? _____

_____

_____

Would I recommend this book? Why or Why not? _____

_____

_____

If so, to whom? _____

_____

What was the best quote or idea I got from this book? _____

_____

_____

_____

_____

If someone challenged this book, what reason do I *think* they would give? _____

_____

_____

_____

_____

Has it been challenged? If so, was it banned, and for what reason? _____

_____

_____

_____

_____

_____

What would I say to people who want to ban this book? _____

_____

_____

_____

_____

_____

_____

My Outlaw Library: Book #34

"Freedom cannot be legislated into existence...freedom cannot be censored into existence."

—Dwight D. Eisenhower, 34th President of the U.S. (1890–1969)

BOOK_____

AUTHOR_____

GENRE_____ DATE FINISHED_____

RATE THE FOLLOWING (1–10):

Characters _____ Plot/Narrative _____ Illustrations (if applicable) _____

HOW I READ IT   ☐ Print   ☐ Audiobook   ☐ eBook

WHERE I GOT IT   ☐ Bookstore   ☐ Library   ☐ Friend   ☐ Other

MOODS/VIBES

1._____
2._____
3._____
4._____
5._____

REPRESENTATION

☐ BIPOC ☐ LGBTQIA+ ☐ Immigrant ☐ Disability ☐ Neurodiversity ☐ Other_____

ASK YOURSELF

What made me pick up this book? _____

_____

_____

_____

_____

Did it deliver? How so? _____

_____

_____

Would I recommend this book? Why or Why not? _____

_____

_____

If so, to whom? _____

_____

What was the best quote or idea I got from this book? _____

_____

_____

_____

_____

If someone challenged this book, what reason do I *think* they would give? _____

_____

_____

_____

Has it been challenged? If so, was it banned, and for what reason? _____

_____

_____

_____

_____

What would I say to people who want to ban this book? _____

_____

_____

_____

_____

_____

_____

My Outlaw Library: Book #35
Banning books is an early sign of authoritarianism.

BOOK_____

AUTHOR_____

GENRE_____ DATE FINISHED_____

RATE THE FOLLOWING (1–10):

Characters _____ Plot/Narrative _____ Illustrations (if applicable) _____

HOW I READ IT ☐ Print ☐ Audiobook ☐ eBook

WHERE I GOT IT ☐ Bookstore ☐ Library ☐ Friend ☐ Other

MOODS/VIBES

1._____

2._____

3._____

4._____

5._____

REPRESENTATION

☐ BIPOC ☐ LGBTQIA+ ☐ Immigrant ☐ Disability ☐ Neurodiversity ☐ Other_____

ASK YOURSELF

What made me pick up this book? _____

_____

_____

_____

_____

Did it deliver? How so? _____

_____

_____

Would I recommend this book? Why or Why not? _____

_____

_____

If so, to whom? _____

_____

What was the best quote or idea I got from this book? _____

_____

_____

_____

_____

_____

If someone challenged this book, what reason do I *think* they would give? _____

_____

_____

_____

_____

Has it been challenged? If so, was it banned, and for what reason? _____

_____

_____

_____

_____

_____

What would I say to people who want to ban this book? _____

_____

_____

_____

_____

_____

_____

My Outlaw Library: Book #36
The most likely people to ban books are also the least likely to learn anything from them.

BOOK _____

AUTHOR _____

GENRE _____ DATE FINISHED _____

RATE THE FOLLOWING (1–10):

Characters _____ Plot/Narrative _____ Illustrations (if applicable) _____

HOW I READ IT ☐ Print ☐ Audiobook ☐ eBook

WHERE I GOT IT ☐ Bookstore ☐ Library ☐ Friend ☐ Other

MOODS/VIBES

1. _____

2. _____

3. _____

4. _____

5. _____

REPRESENTATION

☐ BIPOC ☐ LGBTQIA+ ☐ Immigrant ☐ Disability ☐ Neurodiversity ☐ Other_____

ASK YOURSELF

What made me pick up this book? _____

_____

_____

_____

_____

Did it deliver? How so? _____

_____

_____

Would I recommend this book? Why or Why not? _____

_____

_____

If so, to whom? _____

_____

What was the best quote or idea I got from this book? _____

_____

_____

_____

_____

If someone challenged this book, what reason do I *think* they would give? _____

_____

_____

_____

Has it been challenged? If so, was it banned, and for what reason? _____

_____

_____

_____

_____

What would I say to people who want to ban this book? _____

_____

_____

_____

_____

_____

My Outlaw Library: Book #37

"Censorship ends...when nobody is allowed to read any books except the books that nobody reads."

—George Bernard Shaw, Irish playwright and critic (1856–1950)

BOOK_____

AUTHOR_____

GENRE_____ DATE FINISHED_____

RATE THE FOLLOWING (1–10):

Characters _____ Plot/Narrative _____ Illustrations (if applicable) _____

HOW I READ IT ☐ Print ☐ Audiobook ☐ eBook

WHERE I GOT IT ☐ Bookstore ☐ Library ☐ Friend ☐ Other

MOODS/VIBES

1._____

2._____

3._____

4._____

5._____

REPRESENTATION

☐ BIPOC ☐ LGBTQIA+ ☐ Immigrant ☐ Disability ☐ Neurodiversity ☐ Other_____

ASK YOURSELF

What made me pick up this book? _____

_____

_____

_____

_____

Did it deliver? How so? _____

_____

_____

Would I recommend this book? Why or Why not? _____

_____

_____

If so, to whom? _____

_____

What was the best quote or idea I got from this book? _____

_____

_____

_____

_____

If someone challenged this book, what reason do I *think* they would give? _____

_____

_____

_____

_____

Has it been challenged? If so, was it banned, and for what reason? _____

_____

_____

_____

_____

_____

What would I say to people who want to ban this book? _____

_____

_____

_____

_____

_____

_____

My Outlaw Library: Book #38

You can burn any book you'd like, but ideas are incombustible.

BOOK_____

AUTHOR_____

GENRE_____ DATE FINISHED_____

RATE THE FOLLOWING (1–10):

Characters _____ Plot/Narrative _____ Illustrations (if applicable) _____

HOW I READ IT   □ Print   □ Audiobook   □ eBook

WHERE I GOT IT   □ Bookstore   □ Library   □ Friend   □ Other

MOODS/VIBES

1._____
2._____
3._____
4._____
5._____

REPRESENTATION

□ BIPOC □ LGBTQIA+ □ Immigrant □ Disability □ Neurodiversity □ Other_____

ASK YOURSELF

What made me pick up this book? _____

_____

_____

_____

_____

Did it deliver? How so? _____

_____

Would I recommend this book? Why or Why not? _____

_____

If so, to whom? _____

What was the best quote or idea I got from this book? _____

_____

_____

_____

_____

If someone challenged this book, what reason do I *think* they would give? _____

_____

_____

_____

Has it been challenged? If so, was it banned, and for what reason? _____

_____

_____

_____

_____

What would I say to people who want to ban this book? _____

_____

_____

_____

_____

_____

My Outlaw Library: Book #39

Because the only ban should be on bigots and book burners.

BOOK_____

AUTHOR_____

GENRE_____ DATE FINISHED_____

RATE THE FOLLOWING (1–10):

Characters _____ Plot/Narrative _____ Illustrations (if applicable) _____

HOW I READ IT ☐ Print ☐ Audiobook ☐ eBook

WHERE I GOT IT ☐ Bookstore ☐ Library ☐ Friend ☐ Other

MOODS/VIBES

1._____

2._____

3._____

4._____

5._____

REPRESENTATION

☐ BIPOC ☐ LGBTQIA+ ☐ Immigrant ☐ Disability ☐ Neurodiversity ☐ Other_____

ASK YOURSELF

What made me pick up this book? _____

_____

_____

_____

_____

Did it deliver? How so? _____

_____

_____

Would I recommend this book? Why or Why not? _____

_____

_____

If so, to whom? _____

_____

What was the best quote or idea I got from this book? _____

_____

_____

_____

_____

_____

If someone challenged this book, what reason do I *think* they would give? _____

_____

_____

_____

_____

Has it been challenged? If so, was it banned, and for what reason? _____

_____

_____

_____

_____

_____

What would I say to people who want to ban this book? _____

_____

_____

_____

_____

_____

_____

ADD YOUR OWN ENTRIES

Which other books under scrutiny need to be stood up for?

TITLE: _____

AUTHOR: _____

TITLE: _____

AUTHOR: _____

TITLE: _____

AUTHOR: _____

TITLE: _____

AUTHOR: _____

TITLE: _____

AUTHOR: _____

TITLE: _____

AUTHOR: _____

TITLE: _____

AUTHOR: _____

TITLE: _____

AUTHOR: _____

TITLE: _____

AUTHOR: _____

TITLE: _____

AUTHOR: _____

TITLE: _____
AUTHOR: _____

TITLE: _____
AUTHOR: _____

TITLE: _____
AUTHOR: _____

TITLE: _____
AUTHOR: _____

TITLE: _____
AUTHOR: _____

TITLE: _____
AUTHOR: _____

TITLE: _____
AUTHOR: _____

TITLE: _____
AUTHOR: _____

TITLE: _____
AUTHOR: _____

TITLE: _____
AUTHOR: _____

There is more than one way to burn a book. And the world is full of people running about with lit matches.

Ray Bradbury, *Fahrenheit 451*

Censorship is telling a man he can't have a steak just because a baby can't chew it.

Mark Twain

My Outlaw Library: Book #40
I read this banned book and all I got was context, nuance and perspective.

BOOK_____

AUTHOR_____

GENRE_____ DATE FINISHED_____

RATE THE FOLLOWING (1–10):

Characters _____ Plot/Narrative _____ Illustrations (if applicable) _____

HOW I READ IT ☐ Print ☐ Audiobook ☐ eBook

WHERE I GOT IT ☐ Bookstore ☐ Library ☐ Friend ☐ Other

MOODS/VIBES

1._____

2._____

3._____

4._____

5._____

REPRESENTATION

☐ BIPOC ☐ LGBTQIA+ ☐ Immigrant ☐ Disability ☐ Neurodiversity ☐ Other_____

ASK YOURSELF

What made me pick up this book? _____

_____

_____

_____

_____

Did it deliver? How so? _____

_____

Would I recommend this book? Why or Why not? _____

_____

If so, to whom? _____

What was the best quote or idea I got from this book? _____

_____

_____

_____

_____

If someone challenged this book, what reason do I *think* they would give? ___

_____

_____

_____

Has it been challenged? If so, was it banned, and for what reason? _____

_____

_____

_____

_____

What would I say to people who want to ban this book? _____

_____

_____

_____

_____

_____

_____

My Outlaw Library: Book #41
Their fear will never replace your curiosity, determination or empathy.

BOOK_____

AUTHOR_____

GENRE_____ DATE FINISHED_____

RATE THE FOLLOWING (1–10):

Characters _____ Plot/Narrative _____ Illustrations (if applicable) _____

HOW I READ IT   ☐ Print   ☐ Audiobook   ☐ eBook

WHERE I GOT IT   ☐ Bookstore   ☐ Library   ☐ Friend   ☐ Other

MOODS/VIBES

1._____

2._____

3._____

4._____

5._____

REPRESENTATION

☐ BIPOC ☐ LGBTQIA+ ☐ Immigrant ☐ Disability ☐ Neurodiversity ☐ Other_____

ASK YOURSELF

What made me pick up this book? _____

_____

_____

_____

_____

Did it deliver? How so? _____

_____

_____

Would I recommend this book? Why or Why not? _____

_____

_____

If so, to whom? _____

_____

What was the best quote or idea I got from this book? _____

_____

_____

_____

_____

If someone challenged this book, what reason do I *think* they would give? _____

_____

_____

_____

Has it been challenged? If so, was it banned, and for what reason? _____

_____

_____

_____

_____

What would I say to people who want to ban this book? _____

_____

_____

_____

_____

_____

_____

My Outlaw Library: Book #42

Because when history looks back on book burners, it's never in a good light.

BOOK _____

AUTHOR _____

GENRE _____ DATE FINISHED _____

RATE THE FOLLOWING (1–10):

Characters _____ Plot/Narrative _____ Illustrations (if applicable) _____

HOW I READ IT □ Print □ Audiobook □ eBook

WHERE I GOT IT □ Bookstore □ Library □ Friend □ Other

MOODS/VIBES

1. _____
2. _____
3. _____
4. _____
5. _____

REPRESENTATION

□ BIPOC □ LGBTQIA+ □ Immigrant □ Disability □ Neurodiversity □ Other_____

ASK YOURSELF

What made me pick up this book? _____

_____

_____

_____

_____

Did it deliver? How so? _____

_____

_____

Would I recommend this book? Why or Why not? _____

_____

_____

If so, to whom? _____

What was the best quote or idea I got from this book? _____

_____

_____

_____

_____

_____

If someone challenged this book, what reason do I *think* they would give? _____

_____

_____

_____

Has it been challenged? If so, was it banned, and for what reason? _____

_____

_____

_____

_____

_____

What would I say to people who want to ban this book? _____

_____

_____

_____

_____

_____

_____

My Outlaw Library: Book #43

"[Censorship] is a brand on the imagination that affects the individual who has suffered it, forever."
—Nadine Gordimer, South African writer (1923–2014)

BOOK_____

AUTHOR_____

GENRE_____ DATE FINISHED_____

RATE THE FOLLOWING (1–10):

Characters _____ Plot/Narrative _____ Illustrations (if applicable) _____

HOW I READ IT ☐ Print ☐ Audiobook ☐ eBook

WHERE I GOT IT ☐ Bookstore ☐ Library ☐ Friend ☐ Other

MOODS/VIBES

1._____

2._____

3._____

4._____

5._____

REPRESENTATION

☐ BIPOC ☐ LGBTQIA+ ☐ Immigrant ☐ Disability ☐ Neurodiversity ☐ Other_____

ASK YOURSELF

What made me pick up this book? _____

_____

_____

_____

_____

Did it deliver? How so? _____

_____

_____

Would I recommend this book? Why or Why not? _____

_____

_____

If so, to whom? _____

_____

What was the best quote or idea I got from this book? _____

_____

_____

_____

_____

_____

If someone challenged this book, what reason do I *think* they would give? _____

_____

_____

_____

_____

Has it been challenged? If so, was it banned, and for what reason? _____

_____

_____

_____

_____

_____

What would I say to people who want to ban this book? _____

_____

_____

_____

_____

_____

My Outlaw Library: Book #44
Read like your rights depend on it.

BOOK _____

AUTHOR _____

GENRE _____ DATE FINISHED _____

RATE THE FOLLOWING (1–10):

Characters _____ Plot/Narrative _____ Illustrations (if applicable) _____

HOW I READ IT ☐ Print ☐ Audiobook ☐ eBook

WHERE I GOT IT ☐ Bookstore ☐ Library ☐ Friend ☐ Other

MOODS/VIBES

1. _____
2. _____
3. _____
4. _____
5. _____

REPRESENTATION

☐ BIPOC ☐ LGBTQIA+ ☐ Immigrant ☐ Disability ☐ Neurodiversity ☐ Other_____

ASK YOURSELF

What made me pick up this book? _____

_____

_____

_____

_____

Did it deliver? How so? _____

_____

_____

Would I recommend this book? Why or Why not? _____

_____

_____

If so, to whom? _____

_____

What was the best quote or idea I got from this book? _____

_____

_____

_____

_____

If someone challenged this book, what reason do I *think* they would give? _____

_____

_____

_____

Has it been challenged? If so, was it banned, and for what reason? _____

_____

_____

_____

_____

What would I say to people who want to ban this book? _____

_____

_____

_____

_____

_____

My Outlaw Library: Book #45

Every banned book guides you to something they're afraid of you finding out.

BOOK_____

AUTHOR_____

GENRE_____ DATE FINISHED_____

RATE THE FOLLOWING (1–10):

Characters _____ Plot/Narrative _____ Illustrations (if applicable) _____

HOW I READ IT ☐ Print ☐ Audiobook ☐ eBook

WHERE I GOT IT ☐ Bookstore ☐ Library ☐ Friend ☐ Other

MOODS/VIBES

1._____
2._____
3._____
4._____
5._____

REPRESENTATION

☐ BIPOC ☐ LGBTQIA+ ☐ Immigrant ☐ Disability ☐ Neurodiversity ☐ Other_____

ASK YOURSELF

What made me pick up this book? _____

_____

_____

_____

_____

Did it deliver? How so? _____

_____

_____

Would I recommend this book? Why or Why not? _____

_____

_____

If so, to whom? _____

_____

What was the best quote or idea I got from this book? _____

_____

_____

_____

_____

_____

If someone challenged this book, what reason do I *think* they would give? _____

_____

_____

_____

_____

Has it been challenged? If so, was it banned, and for what reason? _____

_____

_____

_____

_____

_____

What would I say to people who want to ban this book? _____

_____

_____

_____

_____

_____

_____

My Outlaw Library: Book #46

You can censor, ban or even burn books.
But the ideas they contain can be eternal, with your help.

BOOK_____

AUTHOR_____

GENRE_____ DATE FINISHED_____

RATE THE FOLLOWING (1–10):

Characters _____ Plot/Narrative _____ Illustrations (if applicable) _____

HOW I READ IT ☐ Print ☐ Audiobook ☐ eBook

WHERE I GOT IT ☐ Bookstore ☐ Library ☐ Friend ☐ Other

MOODS/VIBES

1._____

2._____

3._____

4._____

5._____

REPRESENTATION

☐ BIPOC ☐ LGBTQIA+ ☐ Immigrant ☐ Disability ☐ Neurodiversity ☐ Other_____

ASK YOURSELF

What made me pick up this book? _____

_____

_____

_____

_____

Did it deliver? How so? _____

_____

_____

Would I recommend this book? Why or Why not? _____

_____

_____

If so, to whom? _____

_____

What was the best quote or idea I got from this book? _____

_____

_____

_____

_____

_____

If someone challenged this book, what reason do I *think* they would give? _____

_____

_____

_____

_____

Has it been challenged? If so, was it banned, and for what reason? _____

_____

_____

_____

_____

_____

What would I say to people who want to ban this book? _____

_____

_____

_____

_____

_____

_____

My Outlaw Library: Book #47
Read this book to trigger the right-wing snowflakes.

BOOK_____

AUTHOR_____

GENRE_____ DATE FINISHED_____

RATE THE FOLLOWING (1–10):

Characters _____ Plot/Narrative _____ Illustrations (if applicable) _____

HOW I READ IT ☐ Print ☐ Audiobook ☐ eBook

WHERE I GOT IT ☐ Bookstore ☐ Library ☐ Friend ☐ Other

MOODS/VIBES

1._____

2._____

3._____

4._____

5._____

REPRESENTATION

☐ BIPOC ☐ LGBTQIA+ ☐ Immigrant ☐ Disability ☐ Neurodiversity ☐ Other_____

ASK YOURSELF

What made me pick up this book? _____

_____

_____

_____

_____

Did it deliver? How so? _____

_____

_____

Would I recommend this book? Why or Why not? _____

_____

_____

If so, to whom? _____

_____

What was the best quote or idea I got from this book? _____

_____

_____

_____

_____

_____

If someone challenged this book, what reason do I *think* they would give? _____

_____

_____

_____

_____

Has it been challenged? If so, was it banned, and for what reason? _____

_____

_____

_____

_____

_____

What would I say to people who want to ban this book? _____

_____

_____

_____

_____

_____

_____

My Outlaw Library: Book #48

Because no power is above the censure of the written word.

BOOK_____

AUTHOR_____

GENRE_____ DATE FINISHED_____

RATE THE FOLLOWING (1–10):

Characters _____ Plot/Narrative _____ Illustrations (if applicable) _____

HOW I READ IT   ☐ Print   ☐ Audiobook   ☐ eBook

WHERE I GOT IT   ☐ Bookstore   ☐ Library   ☐ Friend   ☐ Other

MOODS/VIBES

1._____

2._____

3._____

4._____

5._____

REPRESENTATION

☐ BIPOC ☐ LGBTQIA+ ☐ Immigrant ☐ Disability ☐ Neurodiversity ☐ Other_____

ASK YOURSELF

What made me pick up this book? _____

_____

_____

_____

_____

Did it deliver? How so? _____

_____

Would I recommend this book? Why or Why not? _____

_____

If so, to whom? _____

What was the best quote or idea I got from this book? _____

_____

_____

_____

_____

If someone challenged this book, what reason do I *think* they would give? _____

_____

_____

_____

Has it been challenged? If so, was it banned, and for what reason? _____

_____

_____

_____

_____

What would I say to people who want to ban this book? _____

_____

_____

_____

_____

_____

_____

My Outlaw Library: Book #49

"When decorum is repression, the only dignity free people have is to speak out."
—Abbie Hoffman, American activist (1936–1989)

BOOK_____

AUTHOR_____

GENRE_____ DATE FINISHED_____

RATE THE FOLLOWING (1–10):

Characters _____ Plot/Narrative _____ Illustrations (if applicable) _____

HOW I READ IT ☐ Print ☐ Audiobook ☐ eBook

WHERE I GOT IT ☐ Bookstore ☐ Library ☐ Friend ☐ Other

MOODS/VIBES

1._____

2._____

3._____

4._____

5._____

REPRESENTATION

☐ BIPOC ☐ LGBTQIA+ ☐ Immigrant ☐ Disability ☐ Neurodiversity ☐ Other_____

ASK YOURSELF

What made me pick up this book? _____

_____

_____

_____

_____

Did it deliver? How so? _____

_____

_____

Would I recommend this book? Why or Why not? _____

_____

_____

If so, to whom? _____

_____

What was the best quote or idea I got from this book? _____

_____

_____

_____

_____

_____

If someone challenged this book, what reason do I *think* they would give? _____

_____

_____

_____

Has it been challenged? If so, was it banned, and for what reason? _____

_____

_____

_____

_____

What would I say to people who want to ban this book? _____

_____

_____

_____

_____

_____

_____

Voices of the People
Question 4: Reinforcement

In my interviews with real folks impacted by book challenges,
I found fright, outrage and anger, but also a bit of hope (thanks, students!)
In Part 4, we discuss the following question:

What is something you'd like to tell an author whose book has been challenged/banned?

Your work is essential, especially to marginalized students. That's why I'll keep fighting to keep those books on our shelves.

—Jeff, Teacher

To be honest, I'm not sure, but I know I'd be extremely sympathetic toward them. They didn't do anything wrong, and the book that they worked very hard on can no longer be enjoyed by other people. It's downright infuriating. Let people share their beliefs and opinions. It's okay that their views aren't the same as yours. Diversity is crucial to any society.

—Ainslee Flanagan, Student

Jodi Picoult, George M. Johnson and Judy Blume—THANK YOU for your efforts to support schools and libraries against book bans.

—Anonymous Library Media Director, Lowell Area Schools

I'd like to tell them to keep writing! If your book has been challenged or banned, it's a good sign that it has had a positive impact already and is a much-needed book.

—Emily Lessig, The Violet Fox Bookshop, Virginia

They should be honored that their book was different enough to be noticed and thought-provoking enough to challenge. However, they should also be outraged and fight for their ideas.

—V. Marsh, Student

For those whose books are autobiographical, I am so sorry. You have a right to share your life and story and having your identity banned must be so painful.

—Holly C., Parent, Michigan

To the person who wrote *Charlotte's Web*, I'm so sorry that your book got banned. It was a stupid reason but a really good book!

—Anneliese, Student

I'd like to tell Maia Kobabe that eir book *Gender Queer* saved my life. It made me feel seen. I know the banners feel so threatened by that because trans people challenge them, but we do exist, and we'll keep writing and reading books for us, by us. I'd just like to thank Maia for being incredible and say I'm sorry ey're being targeted.

—Anna, Teacher

My Outlaw Library: Book #50

May the last book ban you read about be the LAST book ban.

BOOK _____

AUTHOR _____

GENRE _____ DATE FINISHED _____

RATE THE FOLLOWING (1–10):

Characters _____ Plot/Narrative _____ Illustrations (if applicable) _____

HOW I READ IT ☐ Print ☐ Audiobook ☐ eBook

WHERE I GOT IT ☐ Bookstore ☐ Library ☐ Friend ☐ Other

MOODS/VIBES

1. _____
2. _____
3. _____
4. _____
5. _____

REPRESENTATION

☐ BIPOC ☐ LGBTQIA+ ☐ Immigrant ☐ Disability ☐ Neurodiversity ☐ Other_____

ASK YOURSELF

What made me pick up this book? _____

_____

_____

_____

_____

Did it deliver? How so? _____

_____

Would I recommend this book? Why or Why not? _____

_____

If so, to whom? _____

What was the best quote or idea I got from this book? _____

_____

_____

_____

_____

If someone challenged this book, what reason do I *think* they would give? ____

_____

_____

_____

Has it been challenged? If so, was it banned, and for what reason? _____

_____

_____

_____

_____

What would I say to people who want to ban this book? _____

_____

_____

_____

_____

_____

_____

Censorship is the child of fear and the father of ignorance.

Laurie Halse Anderson, *Speak*

Something will be offensive to someone in every book, so you've got to fight it.

Judy Blume

My Outlaw Library: Book #51
Because banned book lists are good for one thing: compiling the interesting and informative

BOOK_____

AUTHOR_____

GENRE_____ DATE FINISHED_____

RATE THE FOLLOWING (1–10):

Characters _____ Plot/Narrative _____ Illustrations (if applicable) _____

HOW I READ IT ☐ Print   ☐ Audiobook   ☐ eBook

WHERE I GOT IT ☐ Bookstore   ☐ Library   ☐ Friend   ☐ Other

MOODS/VIBES

1._____

2._____

3._____

4._____

5._____

REPRESENTATION

☐ BIPOC ☐ LGBTQIA+ ☐ Immigrant ☐ Disability ☐ Neurodiversity ☐ Other_____

ASK YOURSELF

What made me pick up this book? _____

_____

_____

_____

_____

Did it deliver? How so? _____

_____

_____

Would I recommend this book? Why or Why not? _____

_____

_____

If so, to whom? _____

_____

What was the best quote or idea I got from this book? _____

_____

_____

_____

_____

_____

If someone challenged this book, what reason do I *think* they would give? _____

_____

_____

_____

_____

Has it been challenged? If so, was it banned, and for what reason? _____

_____

_____

_____

_____

_____

What would I say to people who want to ban this book? _____

_____

_____

_____

_____

_____

_____

My Outlaw Library: Book #52
Because they can't censor curiosity

BOOK _____

AUTHOR _____

GENRE _____ DATE FINISHED _____

RATE THE FOLLOWING (1–10):

Characters _____ Plot/Narrative _____ Illustrations (if applicable) _____

HOW I READ IT ☐ Print ☐ Audiobook ☐ eBook

WHERE I GOT IT ☐ Bookstore ☐ Library ☐ Friend ☐ Other

MOODS/VIBES

1. _____

2. _____

3. _____

4. _____

5. _____

REPRESENTATION

☐ BIPOC ☐ LGBTQIA+ ☐ Immigrant ☐ Disability ☐ Neurodiversity ☐ Other_____

ASK YOURSELF

What made me pick up this book? _____

_____

_____

_____

_____

Did it deliver? How so? _____

_____

_____

Would I recommend this book? Why or Why not? _____

_____

_____

If so, to whom? _____

_____

What was the best quote or idea I got from this book? _____

_____

_____

_____

_____

If someone challenged this book, what reason do I *think* they would give? _____

_____

_____

_____

_____

Has it been challenged? If so, was it banned, and for what reason? _____

_____

_____

_____

_____

_____

What would I say to people who want to ban this book? _____

_____

_____

_____

_____

_____

_____

My Outlaw Library: Book #53
Remember: You can't criminalize an idea.

BOOK _____

AUTHOR _____

GENRE _____ DATE FINISHED _____

RATE THE FOLLOWING (1–10):

Characters _____ Plot/Narrative _____ Illustrations (if applicable) _____

HOW I READ IT ☐ Print ☐ Audiobook ☐ eBook

WHERE I GOT IT ☐ Bookstore ☐ Library ☐ Friend ☐ Other

MOODS/VIBES

1. _____
2. _____
3. _____
4. _____
5. _____

REPRESENTATION

☐ BIPOC ☐ LGBTQIA+ ☐ Immigrant ☐ Disability ☐ Neurodiversity ☐ Other_____

ASK YOURSELF

What made me pick up this book? _____

_____

_____

_____

_____

Did it deliver? How so? _____

_____

_____

Would I recommend this book? Why or Why not? _____

_____

_____

If so, to whom? _____

_____

What was the best quote or idea I got from this book? _____

_____

_____

_____

_____

_____

If someone challenged this book, what reason do I *think* they would give? _____

_____

_____

_____

_____

Has it been challenged? If so, was it banned, and for what reason? _____

_____

_____

_____

_____

_____

What would I say to people who want to ban this book? _____

_____

_____

_____

_____

_____

_____

Voices of the People
Question 5: Bottom Line

In my interviews with real folks impacted by book challenges,
I found fright, outrage and anger, but also a bit of hope (thanks, students!)
In Part 5, we discuss the following question:

Booksellers and librarians play a special role in the fight against book bans. What are your thoughts?

Just because they don't agree with or like a book doesn't mean they have the right to take it away from everyone else. Not everyone has the same beliefs. It's important, as educators, to be able to use books to provide mirrors, windows and sliding glass door opportunities to our students.

—Christi,
Retired Teacher/Bookseller

While everyone in our community has some responsibility to fight censorship, we have a bit more power to make change than most because we have a platform to speak out on social media, we have the power to curate books for our communities, and we have the opportunity to use our bookstores as a place of education, discussion and growth.

—Emily Lessig,
The Violet Fox Bookshop

The book challenges we've seen have been more in the political realm than in the act of requests for reevaluation.... [They] engender mistrust between frontline staff and those in administration, making it harder to run successful initiatives in our libraries.

—Erin, Librarian

The year I had my challenge was soul-crushing. I thought about quitting my job. I felt like I completely lost faith in my administrators and district.

—Anonymous Librarian

We become educators and smugglers, ensuring the books are still available and encouraged, along with other books that widen our worldview.

—Aimee, Bookseller

I don't actually believe all of this nonsense has anything to do with the actual books. I believe it is all about control and creating chaos in public schools. I think they are using schools as a pawn in their political games and want to foster fear in their followers and create mistrust of public school educators by creating this false narrative that we are bad people.

—Anonymous Library Media Director, Lowell Area Schools

My Outlaw Library: Book #54

Be like LaVar Burton: always ready to throw hands with Moms for Liberty.

BOOK_____

AUTHOR_____

GENRE_____ DATE FINISHED_____

RATE THE FOLLOWING (1–10):

Characters _____   Plot/Narrative _____   Illustrations (if applicable) _____

HOW I READ IT   ☐ Print   ☐ Audiobook   ☐ eBook

WHERE I GOT IT   ☐ Bookstore   ☐ Library   ☐ Friend   ☐ Other

MOODS/VIBES

1._____

2._____

3._____

4._____

5._____

REPRESENTATION

☐ BIPOC ☐ LGBTQIA+ ☐ Immigrant ☐ Disability ☐ Neurodiversity ☐ Other_____

ASK YOURSELF

What made me pick up this book? _____

_____

_____

_____

_____

Did it deliver? How so? _____

_____

_____

Would I recommend this book? Why or Why not? _____

_____

_____

If so, to whom? _____

_____

What was the best quote or idea I got from this book? _____

_____

_____

_____

_____

_____

If someone challenged this book, what reason do I *think* they would give? _____

_____

_____

_____

_____

Has it been challenged? If so, was it banned, and for what reason? _____

_____

_____

_____

_____

_____

What would I say to people who want to ban this book? _____

_____

_____

_____

_____

_____

_____

My Outlaw Library: Book #55

Because book banners are always on the wrong side of history.

BOOK _____

AUTHOR _____

GENRE _____ DATE FINISHED _____

RATE THE FOLLOWING (1–10):

Characters _____ Plot/Narrative _____ Illustrations (if applicable) _____

HOW I READ IT ☐ Print ☐ Audiobook ☐ eBook

WHERE I GOT IT ☐ Bookstore ☐ Library ☐ Friend ☐ Other

MOODS/VIBES

1. _____
2. _____
3. _____
4. _____
5. _____

REPRESENTATION

☐ BIPOC ☐ LGBTQIA+ ☐ Immigrant ☐ Disability ☐ Neurodiversity ☐ Other_____

ASK YOURSELF

What made me pick up this book? _____

_____

_____

_____

_____

Did it deliver? How so? _____

_____

_____

Would I recommend this book? Why or Why not? _____

_____

_____

If so, to whom? _____

_____

What was the best quote or idea I got from this book? _____

_____

_____

_____

_____

_____

If someone challenged this book, what reason do I *think* they would give? _____

_____

_____

_____

_____

Has it been challenged? If so, was it banned, and for what reason? _____

_____

_____

_____

_____

_____

What would I say to people who want to ban this book? _____

_____

_____

_____

_____

_____

_____

My Outlaw Library: Book #56
Don't worry: the right is just jealous of your reading comprehension skills.

BOOK_____

AUTHOR_____

GENRE_____ DATE FINISHED_____

RATE THE FOLLOWING (1–10):

Characters _____ Plot/Narrative _____ Illustrations (if applicable) _____

HOW I READ IT ☐ Print ☐ Audiobook ☐ eBook

WHERE I GOT IT ☐ Bookstore ☐ Library ☐ Friend ☐ Other

MOODS/VIBES

1._____
2._____
3._____
4._____
5._____

REPRESENTATION

☐ BIPOC ☐ LGBTQIA+ ☐ Immigrant ☐ Disability ☐ Neurodiversity ☐ Other_____

ASK YOURSELF

What made me pick up this book? _____
_____
_____
_____
_____

Did it deliver? How so? _____

_____

_____

Would I recommend this book? Why or Why not? _____

_____

_____

If so, to whom? _____

_____

What was the best quote or idea I got from this book? _____

_____

_____

_____

_____

If someone challenged this book, what reason do I *think* they would give? _____

_____

_____

_____

Has it been challenged? If so, was it banned, and for what reason? _____

_____

_____

_____

_____

What would I say to people who want to ban this book? _____

_____

_____

_____

_____

_____

Think for yourselves and let others enjoy the privilege to do so, too.

Voltaire, "Treatise on Tolerance"

Books and ideas are the most effective weapons against intolerance and ignorance.

Lyndon B. Johnson

Banished to Vanished

When the bad guys get their way, certain books get culled from county libraries and shops. But do they ever really become impossible to find?

WHEN IT COMES to the question of how to get your hands on books that are no longer widely available in your area due to book bans and challenges, the answer isn't as clear-cut as you might expect. The good news is that because of the hyperlocal nature of book challenges and bans, it's hard to find examples of books that have been successfully banned out of existence.

In fact, a ban can sometimes have the opposite effect. Books that have been banned or challenged regularly become bestsellers due to the publicity associated with the ban itself. But don't get the idea that being banned is great for an author. While this can be true in some high-profile cases, book bans tend to hurt authors overall. Even though the hyper-localization of book ban legislation often allows those in search of a banned book to find one a short distance away, the bans ultimately diminish the platform for that author and those with a similar voice.

Many authors, especially of children's literature, rely heavily on school visits and library sales for their income. When a book is regularly being challenged, school districts and libraries may be hesitant to stock it or invite the author to visit. Publishers may also decide that the potential for lawsuits and bad press from authors who write content that is regularly challenged or banned isn't worth the effort of promoting them. This leads to fewer opportunities for authors, particularly those from marginalized communities who have a harder time being published in the first place.

Librarians, teachers and even booksellers are being threatened with legislation across the country that would hold them personally liable for any books a parent is offended by. The resulting overcaution has an effect on the books they're willing to purchase/stock.

One of the scariest things about book challenges and bans is that they don't lead to books going out of existence: They lead to books never existing in the first place.

The Plan to Unban

So: A book has been banned. What can you do about it? Lots!

1. SHOW UP.

The first thing I always encourage people to do is show up! Go to your library or school board meeting and speak to the passion of books, the importance of free speech and the power of representation. We need to put the same energy that people put into banning books into fighting for their return.

2. REQUEST THE BOOK.

Every library has finite space and dollars to spend on their collection, which means they place a priority on the books that they know people want. So request the book! Every library has a system for patrons to request books that aren't in the collection, so use it!

3. READ THE BOOK.

Before a book is banned or even challenged, go read it! Having the numbers to show that a certain book is desired and being read by the community goes a long way in helping a library justify keeping something in the collection.

4. RUN FOR SOMETHING.

If you've had the unfortunate luck of having book banners overrun your local school or library board, run in the next election. Put yourself in the position to protect our books and support our librarians. At the very least, make sure you're paying attention to your local elections. Ask those running to share their position on the freedom to read, and make sure to be vocal in your support or opposition to those candidates.

5. LIGHTS, CAMERA, TAKE ACTION.

Don't forget to call for backup. Get the media involved. Bring attention to the situation through social media, letters to the editor and your local news networks. Contact your state library association, the American Library Association, the ACLU and other organizations dedicated to your right to read. They all have the expertise and resources to help!

I Got Banned For That?!

In my opinion, there is truly no good rationale for banning books, but sometimes the reasons people give for wanting to ban a book are beyond bad.

THE MERRIAM-WEBSTER DICTIONARY

BANNED FOR: SEXUALLY GRAPHIC EXPLANATION OF ORAL SEX

California school district parents objected to the dictionary being in their kids' classrooms due to the "graphic" nature of its explanations of oral sex and other terms.

BROWN BEAR, BROWN BEAR, WHAT DID YOU SEE?

by Bill Martin Jr.

BANNED FOR: A CASE OF MISTAKEN IDENTITY

Texas officials confused Bill Martin Jr., the author of this classic children's book, with

another Bill Martin, who wrote the book *Ethical Marxism* in 2008...four years after Bill Martin Jr. died.

CHARLOTTE'S WEB

by E.B. White

BANNED FOR: BEING BLASPHEMOUS

In 2006, Kansas parents objected to the classic kids' novel *Charlotte's Web* being in school libraries because they felt that it was blasphemous. According to the group: "humans are the highest level of God's creation and are the only creatures that can communicate vocally. Showing lower life forms with human abilities is sacrilegious and disrespectful to God."

A DAY IN THE LIFE OF MARLON BUNDO

by Jill Twiss

BANNED FOR: BEING "DESIGNED TO POLLUTE THE MORALS OF ITS READERS"

On the ALA top 10 most challenged lists for both 2018 and 2019, *A Day in the Life of Marlon Bundo*—a book about the fanciful adventures of then-vice president Mike Pence's pet rabbit—was challenged for a host of reasons related to LGBTQIA+ content, politics and failing to have a content warning. That, and "pollut[ing] the morals of its readers."

DIARY OF A YOUNG GIRL

by Anne Frank

BANNED FOR: BEING A "REAL DOWNER"

In 1983, the Alabama State Textbook Committee reviewed the classic diary of Frank's time in occupied Amsterdam. Four members recommended rejecting the title because they deemed it "a real downer."

A LIGHT IN THE ATTIC

by Shel Silverstein

BANNED FOR: ENCOURAGING CHILDREN TO BREAK DISHES SO THEY WON'T HAVE TO DRY THEM

Shel Silverstein's classic collection of poems *A Light in the Attic* is a fun read for most elementary students. But parents at a school in Beloit, Wisconsin, successfully challenged the book and got it banned because the poem "How Not to Have to Dry the Dishes" might encourage children to break dishes to avoid this particular chore.

FIFTY SHADES OF GREY

by E.L. James

BANNED FOR: BEING POORLY WRITTEN

Everyone's a critic, but despite your feelings about this racy novel, saying "Laters, baby" to a book and banning it simply because you don't like its writing style is not the answer!

TARZAN

by Edgar Rice Burroughs

BANNED FOR: REPRESENTING COHABITATION WITHOUT MARRIAGE

In 1961, a California elementary school removed Edgar Rice Burroughs's novels after parents complained that Tarzan and Jane, jungle roommates, were never shown to be properly married.

ANTIRACIST BABY

by Ibram X. Kendi

BANNED FOR: BRAINWASHING KIDS INTO BELIEVING "UNMORAL" THINGS

A challenger claimed *Antiracist Baby*, along with *The Little Feminist* series and *Love Makes a Family*, were all aimed at "Brainwashing kids into believing unmoral things. [T]alking about Black lives matters [sic], sexuality at this age is wrong." I disrespectfully disagree.

I SPY FUN HOUSE

BANNED FOR: SCARY CLOWNS

Gladstone Public Library in Gladstone, Michigan, received a challenge for the popular *I Spy* book due to the scary nature of the clowns. While they're not necessarily wrong about the clowns, some people like being scared!

Bookstore Bucket List

The purveyors, small publishers and banned-knowledge pushers to visit on your literary journey.

I MAY BE BIASED, but to me, the best part about checking out a new city is finding the local bookstore!

Bookstore road trips? Always a yes for me!

Make your own bucket list of bookstores you've found out about on social media, through friends or in a news report about folks fighting the good fight against small-mindedness.

NAME _____

LOCATION _____

FOUND VIA _____ DATE VISITED_____

NOTES_____

_____

NAME _____

LOCATION _____

FOUND VIA _____ DATE VISITED_____

NOTES_____

_____

NAME _____

LOCATION _____

FOUND VIA _____ DATE VISITED_____

NOTES_____

_____

NAME _____

LOCATION _____

FOUND VIA _____ DATE VISITED_____

NOTES_____

_____

A one-of-a-kind "unburnable" edition of Margaret Atwood's **The Handmaid's Tale** appeared on the auction block at Sotheby New York in June 2022.

NAME _____

LOCATION _____

FOUND VIA _____ DATE VISITED_____

NOTES_____

_____

NAME _____

LOCATION _____

FOUND VIA _____ DATE VISITED_____

NOTES_____

_____

NAME _____

LOCATION _____

FOUND VIA _____ DATE VISITED_____

NOTES_____

_____

NAME _____

LOCATION _____

FOUND VIA _____ DATE VISITED_____

NOTES_____

_____

NAME _____

LOCATION _____

FOUND VIA _____ DATE VISITED_____

NOTES_____

_____

NAME _____

LOCATION _____

FOUND VIA _____ DATE VISITED_____

NOTES_____

NAME _____

LOCATION _____

FOUND VIA _____ DATE VISITED_____

NOTES_____

NAME _____

LOCATION _____

FOUND VIA _____ DATE VISITED_____

NOTES_____

NAME _____

LOCATION _____

FOUND VIA _____ DATE VISITED_____

NOTES_____

NAME _____

LOCATION _____

FOUND VIA _____ DATE VISITED_____

NOTES_____

NAME _____

LOCATION _____

FOUND VIA _____ DATE VISITED_____

NOTES_____

NAME _____

LOCATION _____

FOUND VIA _____ DATE VISITED_____

NOTES_____

NAME _____

LOCATION _____

FOUND VIA _____ DATE VISITED_____

NOTES_____

NAME _____

LOCATION _____

FOUND VIA _____ DATE VISITED_____

NOTES_____

NAME _____

LOCATION _____

FOUND VIA _____ DATE VISITED_____

NOTES_____

NAME _____

LOCATION _____

FOUND VIA _____ DATE VISITED_____

NOTES_____

NAME _____

LOCATION _____

FOUND VIA _____ DATE VISITED_____

NOTES_____

NAME _____

LOCATION _____

FOUND VIA _____ DATE VISITED_____

NOTES_____

NAME _____

LOCATION _____

FOUND VIA _____ DATE VISITED_____

NOTES_____

My Most "Dangerous" Reads
Most people don't realize their bookshelves at home already contain banned books.

LET'S LOOK AT your favorite books and see if they've been banned or challenged: Odds are, you'll be surprised by the answer. Fill in the title, then note the most common reasons given for challenging or banning the book to create a full account of the outlaw library additions you already have on your shelves.

Check the American Library Association or PEN America websites to see if a book has been banned or challenged or just use the search terms "Is [book title] banned?"

BOOK _____

AUTHOR _____ YEAR PUBLISHED _____

Where was it banned? _____ In what year?_____

What reason was given for banning the book? ☐ BIPOC -centric Narratives ☐ LGBTQIA+

☐ Profanity ☐ Sexual Content ☐ Other_____

Has the ban been successfully fought? _____ If so, where? _____

BOOK _____

AUTHOR _____ YEAR PUBLISHED _____

Where was it banned? _____ In what year?_____

What reason was given for banning the book? ☐ BIPOC -centric Narratives ☐ LGBTQIA+

☐ Profanity ☐ Sexual Content ☐ Other_____

Has the ban been successfully fought? _____ If so, where? _____

BOOK _____

AUTHOR _____ YEAR PUBLISHED _____

Where was it banned? _____ In what year?_____

What reason was given for banning the book? ☐ BIPOC -centric Narratives ☐ LGBTQIA+

☐ Profanity ☐ Sexual Content ☐ Other_____

Has the ban been successfully fought? _____ If so, where? _____

According to the American Library Association, the most challenged book of 2022 was Maia Kobabe's **Gender Queer**, a memoir about what it means to be nonbinary.

BOOK_____

AUTHOR _____ YEAR PUBLISHED _____

Where was it banned? _____ In what year?_____

What reason was given for banning the book? ☐ BIPOC -centric Narratives ☐ LGBTQIA+

☐ Profanity ☐ Sexual Content ☐ Other_____

Has the ban been successfully fought? _____ If so, where? _____

BOOK_____

AUTHOR _____ YEAR PUBLISHED _____

Where was it banned? _____ In what year?_____

What reason was given for banning the book? ☐ BIPOC -centric Narratives ☐ LGBTQIA+

☐ Profanity ☐ Sexual Content ☐ Other_____

Has the ban been successfully fought? _____ If so, where? _____

BOOK_____

AUTHOR _____ YEAR PUBLISHED _____

Where was it banned? _____ In what year?_____

What reason was given for banning the book? ☐ BIPOC -centric Narratives ☐ LGBTQIA+

☐ Profanity ☐ Sexual Content ☐ Other_____

Has the ban been successfully fought? _____ If so, where? _____

BOOK_____

AUTHOR _____ YEAR PUBLISHED _____

Where was it banned? _____ In what year?_____

What reason was given for banning the book? ☐ BIPOC -centric Narratives ☐ LGBTQIA+

☐ Profanity ☐ Sexual Content ☐ Other_____

Has the ban been successfully fought? _____ If so, where? _____

Reader's Action List

If you care about fighting censorship in general and book bans specifically, there are a number of ways you can join the fight for free knowledge.

BOOK BANS TEND to be hyperlocal, but the best plan of action to fight back is fairly universal. Step one? Show up. Don't let the only voices in the room be book banners. Having the following information handy will make it easier to take action immediately. Remember: You don't have to wait for someone to challenge a book. You can show up in support of books at any time.

Each section that follows has a space for you to write out what you'd like to say in person. After attending many public meetings with a lot of public comments, I can confidently say you don't need to worry about sounding silly. Anything you have to say will sound better than some of the rambling, off-the-wall word salads I've heard at town halls in my time.

Not sure what to say? Keep it simple "Hi, my name is_____. I wanted to tell you that I am here in support of the freedom to read and believe that access to books is important for everyone. I hope you'll join me in supporting the First Amendment here in our community."

SCHOOL BOARD

School boards generally make the ultimate decision on book bans and challenges in a school district. These folks are members of the community who've been elected to their position. Each district has different rules for comment time, so be sure to check out the specifics for your district. And no, you don't need to have a kid in the district to get involved! When young people are supported and well-educated, it benefits the entire community.

Meeting Date _____ Name & Title _____

Public Comment _____

_____

_____

Meeting Date _____ Name & Title _____

Public Comment _____

_____

_____

Meeting Date _____ Name & Title _____

Public Comment _____

_____

_____

Meeting Date _____ Name & Title _____

Public Comment _____

_____

_____

Meeting Date _____ Name & Title _____

Public Comment _____

_____

_____

Meeting Date _____ Name & Title _____

Public Comment _____

_____

_____

Meeting Date _____ Name & Title _____

Public Comment _____

_____

_____

Meeting Date _____ Name & Title _____

Public Comment _____

_____

_____

According to the American Library Association, there were 695 attempts to restrict library services and materials between January and August 2023.

Reader's Action List
(continued)

Meeting Date _____ Name & Title _____

Public Comment _____

_____

_____

State Library Association _____

Meeting Date _____ Name & Title _____

Public Comment _____

_____

_____

State Library Association _____

Meeting Date _____ Name & Title _____

Public Comment _____

_____

_____

State Library Association _____

Meeting Date _____ Name & Title _____

Public Comment _____

_____

_____

State Library Association _____

CITY/TOWNSHIP

Representative _____ Anti-Ban? ☐ YES ☐ NO

Contact Information _____

Representative _____ Anti-Ban? ☐ YES ☐ NO

Contact Information _____

Representative _____ Anti-Ban? ☐ YES ☐ NO

Contact Information _____

Representative _____ Anti-Ban? ☐ YES ☐ NO

Contact Information _____

COUNTY

Representative _____ Anti-Ban? ☐ YES ☐ NO

Contact Information _____

Representative _____ Anti-Ban? ☐ YES ☐ NO

Contact Information _____

Representative _____ Anti-Ban? ☐ YES ☐ NO

Contact Information _____

STATE

Representative _____ Anti-Ban? ☐ YES ☐ NO

Contact Information _____

Representative _____ Anti-Ban? ☐ YES ☐ NO

Contact Information _____

My To-Read List

A place to keep track of the latest and greatest books being threatened by the pearl-clutchers of the world.

I F THE BOOKS in your to-read list are anything like mine, you're planning to live for another 200 years. Use this page to keep track of the books that pique your interest as you work through your outlaw library. And most importantly, mark them off as you read them! Celebrate those wins, then add another book to the list. It's fascinating to track how and when we discover books, too. Thanks to BookTok and Bookstagram, I've gotten some really great recommendations, but keep an open mind: You might find your next read anywhere.

TITLE _____

AUTHOR _____ GENRE _____

DISCOVERED VIA _____

READ IT YET?
☐ YES ☐ NO

ENDANGERED?
☐ YES ☐ NO

___

TITLE _____

AUTHOR _____ GENRE _____

DISCOVERED VIA _____

READ IT YET?
☐ YES ☐ NO

ENDANGERED?
☐ YES ☐ NO

___

TITLE _____

AUTHOR _____ GENRE _____

DISCOVERED VIA _____

READ IT YET?
☐ YES ☐ NO

ENDANGERED?
☐ YES ☐ NO

___

TITLE _____

AUTHOR _____ GENRE _____

DISCOVERED VIA _____

READ IT YET?
☐ YES ☐ NO

ENDANGERED?
☐ YES ☐ NO

___

TITLE _____

AUTHOR _____ GENRE _____

DISCOVERED VIA _____

READ IT YET?
☐ YES ☐ NO

ENDANGERED?
☐ YES ☐ NO

___

TITLE _____

AUTHOR _____ GENRE _____

DISCOVERED VIA _____

READ IT YET?
☐ YES ☐ NO

ENDANGERED?
☐ YES ☐ NO

TITLE _____

AUTHOR _____ GENRE _____

DISCOVERED VIA _____

READ IT YET?
☐ YES ☐ NO

ENDANGERED?
☐ YES ☐ NO

TITLE _____

AUTHOR _____ GENRE _____

DISCOVERED VIA _____

READ IT YET?
☐ YES ☐ NO

ENDANGERED?
☐ YES ☐ NO

TITLE _____

AUTHOR _____ GENRE _____

DISCOVERED VIA _____

READ IT YET?
☐ YES ☐ NO

ENDANGERED?
☐ YES ☐ NO

TITLE _____

AUTHOR _____ GENRE _____

DISCOVERED VIA _____

READ IT YET?
☐ YES ☐ NO

ENDANGERED?
☐ YES ☐ NO

TITLE _____

AUTHOR _____ GENRE _____

DISCOVERED VIA _____

READ IT YET?
☐ YES ☐ NO

ENDANGERED?
☐ YES ☐ NO

TITLE _____

AUTHOR _____ GENRE _____

DISCOVERED VIA _____

READ IT YET?
☐ YES ☐ NO

ENDANGERED?
☐ YES ☐ NO

TITLE _____

AUTHOR _____ GENRE _____

DISCOVERED VIA _____

READ IT YET?
☐ YES ☐ NO

ENDANGERED?
☐ YES ☐ NO

TITLE _____

AUTHOR _____ GENRE _____

DISCOVERED VIA _____

READ IT YET?
☐ YES ☐ NO

ENDANGERED?
☐ YES ☐ NO

Acknowledgments

Thank you to Shelby, Alyse and Kate for keeping Bettie's Pages, and me, running smoothly!

Bookstore Squad and Shenanigan Squad, our group chats are a lifeline to me.
Thank you for always being there at all hours of the day and night!

All my love to my people. Thank you for loving me and
encouraging me to pursue all my passions.

And Eamon, this is all your fault.
Thank you for telling me it was OK to quit my job and open a bookstore.
You make it possible for me to do all of this!

About the Author

Nicole Lintemuth is the owner of Bettie's Pages, a mission-driven independent bookstore in Lowell, Michigan, that seeks to cultivate community, empower readers and maintain a welcoming space that is diverse, inclusive and affirming.

Apart from being a passionate reader and defender of banned books, Nicole is also an activist, shop cat mom and slight (read: complete) chaos goblin.